A Short History of West Africa

Book One
AD 1000 to 1800

A Short History of West Africa

Book One
AD 1000 to 1800

T. A. Osae
Headmaster, Prempeh College, Kumasi, Ghana

S. N. Nwabara
Deputy Director, Hansberry Institute of African Studies,
University of Nigeria

University of London Press Ltd

GB SBN 340 07771 9

Second impression 1969
Copyright © 1968 T. A. Osae and S. N. Nwabara
Illustrations copyright © 1968 University of London Press Ltd

University of London Press Ltd
St Paul's House, Warwick Lane, London EC4
Represented in West Africa by
C. M. Kershaw, M.A., P.O. Box 62, Ibadan, Nigeria

Printed and bound in England by
C. Tinling and Co. Ltd, London and Prescot

Preface

This book is based on the first section of the new West African History Syllabus issued by the West African Examinations Council for the General Certificate of Education Ordinary Level examinations. It may, however, be of some interest to the general reader wishing to acquaint himself with the past of the peoples of West Africa and their old civilizations. The notion that African history has little in its own right beyond European activities on the continent is quickly disappearing, and this is healthy for scholarship. The rightful place of African history in studies at school has now been sufficiently recognized not only by Africanists but even by those with but a casual interest in history as a subject.

Except for the last chapter, the book deals almost exclusively with the states and kingdoms of West Africa from medieval times to the end of the eighteenth century. We are under no pretensions whatsoever that these states and kingdoms have received adequate treatment. What we have attempted in this short book is to awaken the student's curiosity about those historical developments of West Africa in preparation for a fuller appreciation of the history of Africa as a whole in later studies. In other words, what is presented here is an introduction to the history of West Africa. No attempt has been made to overstate the claims of the old civilizations represented in the various states and kingdoms discussed. There is hardly any need to do this, for the old African civilizations were sufficiently rich to be able to account for themselves in their own right without the help of any such boost.

It should be stressed that the historical developments raised in this book cannot be isolated from contemporary developments in the rest of the African continent as a whole. Events taking place elsewhere in Africa had tremendous effects on developments in West Africa. Common influences starting from the east along the Nile valley and its neighbourhood are very significant, but unfortunately the knowledge possessed on the question at present is far from adequate. In spite of difficulties of communication posed by desert and forest, West Africa was never an island at any stage of its known history. Considerable movements and contacts went on within West Africa itself and between it and the regions to the north and east.

The teacher who finds himself discussing with his students the material and issues *introduced* in this book should realize that the main sources of history of West Africa are scanty and very often of questionable reliability. His task of evaluating evidence is a delicate one: he will have to do the best he can. Where the legend and myth of the origins of states have been recorded as received through tradition these may be regarded as valuable guides. If this is made clear to the student, possible ridicule and confusion may be avoided.

In conclusion, we should like to place on record our deep appreciation for the advice, criticism and encouragement received from friends and colleagues.

T.A.O.
S.N.N.

Contents

Preface

Part One – the Western Sudan

Part Two – the Southern Forest Region

List of Maps

Acknowledgment

The publisher is grateful to the Press Association Ltd for kind permission to reproduce the photographs on the cover.

Part One: The Western Sudan

1 Influences on developments in the Western Sudan

The land

The Arabs in early times referred to Africa south of the Sahara, the land of the Negro, as *Bilad-as-Sudan,* meaning 'Land of the Blacks'. The Sudan, however, is now the general term applied to the area lying between the Sahara Desert and the tropical African forest, stretching from the Atlantic to the Red Sea coasts. The Sudan is a broad savanna belt several hundreds of miles wide, roughly covering in whole or in part the modern states of Senegal, Mauritania, Mali, Upper Volta, Niger, Northern Nigeria, Chad and the Sudan. The Western Sudan, with which we deal here, is about half this area, and stretches from the Atlantic coast to Lake Chad (Map 1).

The Senegal and Niger Rivers run through a considerable distance of the Western Sudan and have played no small part in the history of this vast area. The two rivers not only afforded a ready and easy means of communication but they also made settled life possible. Their banks have always been fairly well populated. People who lead a settled life soon begin to develop a civilization of their own. No less important for the historical and economic development of the Western Sudan in general in early and medieval times was Wangara, a swampy region between the Senegal and the Niger, which became famous as a rich gold-bearing region. Gold has always played an important part in the lives of men of all ages in history. Wangara produced plenty of gold that promoted a trans-Saharan trade between the Western Sudan and North Africa in medieval times. For many years the Western Sudan remained the main source of the supply of gold of the world. The Lake Chad region to the east attracted wandering tribes from the fringes of the Sahara Desert and, like the Niger and the Senegal, made possible the permanent settlement of concentrated populations. The Lake Chad area was

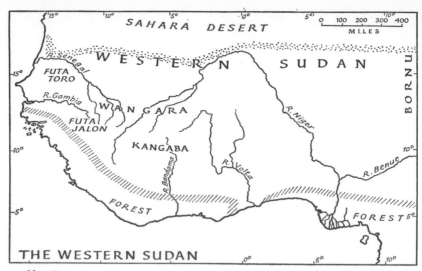

Map 1

important in another way: it was a meeting place between the eastern and western halves of the Sudan.

A good part of the Western Sudan is open country with hardly any remarkable geographical barriers. The open nature of the land was at once a blessing and a curse. It was a blessing because it facilitated contact between the peoples of the area and encouraged the passage of merchandise and ideas. It had a great influence on the development of the great medieval kingdoms or empires of the Western Sudan such as Old Ghana, Mali and Songhai. At the head of a band of mounted warriors the ambitious conqueror could establish control fairly quickly over a wide area and carve an empire for himself. This was what really happened in the Western Sudan, as we shall soon see when we begin to discuss the rise of the medieval kingdoms. However, the same absence of natural barriers which facilitated the building of kingdoms and empires ulti-mately contributed to the disintegration of these kingdoms. The Western Sudanese kingdoms covered more territory than their strength and resources could help them to keep together for a long time. The con-quered territories were never sufficiently welded together into a lasting unit, and the frontiers of the kingdoms always lay open to attack. In the general state of defencelessness created largely by the open nature of the land, kingdoms rose and fell, often quite quickly. At the close of the sixteenth century the Moors from Morocco, once they had mastered the hazards of the Sahara and entered the Western Sudan, invaded and ravaged the heart of Songhai, the leading empire in the Sudan at the time. The Moors ruined the peace and culture of the Western Sudan that had taken centuries to establish. Not long ago, at the end of the nineteenth century, again the open nature of the land in the Western Sudan helped the French to conquer the area and establish former French West Africa.

Contacts between the Western Sudan and the Mediterranean World

Writers of the history of Africa have often enlarged upon the part played by the Sahara Desert in keeping Negro Africa backward for a long time. The Sahara, it has been pointed out, was the main barrier to civilizing agencies from outside, especially from the north. This is to a certain extent correct; but it is a fact also that, from early times, brave traders, religious teachers and adventurous travellers from North Africa dared the hazards of the Sahara and made a regular and most valuable contact between the Mediterranean World and the Western Sudan. The Sahara has always been difficult and dangerous to cross, but it is not all 'sand and sand and sand again'. Parts of it are quite capable of supporting sizeable populations. At various points in the desert are the oases which are fairly well watered and fertile. A carefully selected route passing through a number of oases could successfully take bands of brave travellers from North Africa into the Western Sudan and back. Advantage was taken of this useful fact in early and medieval times. A group of travellers who made the long and risky journey across the desert formed a caravan. In early and medieval times a number of caravan routes linked North Africa and the Western Sudan. Four of these routes were very important and were regularly used.

A western caravan route started from Fez in Morocco, passed through a place called Sijilmasa just outside the desert in the north, and touched the salt-mining town in the desert known by the name Taghaza. From Taghaza the route led to the town of Audaghost in the south-western desert and finally reached Old Ghana in the Western Sudan.* A second caravan route started from Tlemcen in Algeria, passed through a place called Tuat in the desert and reached Timbuktu. A third route in the centre led from Tunis straight down to Gao on the Niger bend through

---

* On attaining independence in 1957 the British West African colony of the Gold Coast adopted the name Ghana for political reasons based on alleged historical ties with the medieval Ghana empire of the Western Sudan.

Ghadames and Aïr, both situated in the central desert. This route was joined at Ghat between Ghadames and Aïr by an auxiliary route running westward from Cairo. Tripoli was linked with the Lake Chad region by a route through Bilma, another salt town in the desert, by way of the Fezzan. If you look at Map 2 you will see the position of these caravan routes.

It should be pointed out that the above description of the caravan routes is a very general one. Emphasis should be placed on the fact that the various routes and their termini in the Western Sudan acquired importance at different times. For example, after the eleventh century Audaghost virtually disappeared from the history of the Western Sudan. Kumbi Saleh, the capital of Ghana, met a similar fate by the end of the thirteenth century. After the disappearance of Kumbi Saleh, Walata became the important terminus of the western route. The famous and almost fabulous Timbuktu did not assume importance as the main entrepôt of the Western Sudan until the fifteenth century. To the east the routes converging on Hausaland did not achieve much commercial value until the seventeenth century, after the Moroccans had invaded and ruined the general stability and commercial prosperity of the Upper Niger from the end of the sixteenth century.

The most important of these caravan routes appear to have been the two in the west that converged on Timbuktu. The route from Tripoli to

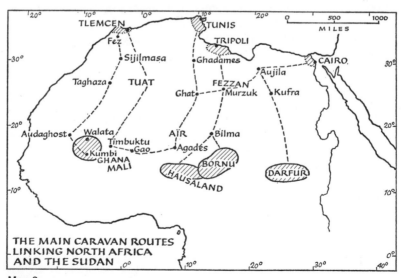

Map 2

Bornu to the east was always of some importance also. Along these routes passed the bulk of the trans-Saharan trade that flourished in medieval times. The Fez–Taghaza–Timbuktu route was pre-eminent as a trade route but was of special importance as a channel through which North African culture reached the Western Sudan. Throughout medieval times Arab traders using the caravan routes entered the Western Sudan and bartered goods for slaves and such Sudanese products as gold, ivory and ostrich feathers. The most valuable article of trade that the Arabs carried to the Sudan was salt, a commodity that was in great demand by the Western Sudanese. They also brought cloths, beads, dried dates and, in later times, firearms. The trade goods that entered the Sudan, needed as they may have been, were not as important in them- selves as the cultural influences that accompanied the trans-Saharan trade. Western Sudanese towns like Kumbi, Audaghost, Jenne, Gao and Timbuktu that featured prominently in the trans-Saharan trade acquired considerably high cultural attainments, partly North African. Some of the North African merchants settled in the towns of the Western Sudan, and these, together with native Sudanese who had grown wealthy through trade, formed a leisurely class who lived very well. El Bekri, an Arab scholar who lived in the eleventh century and to whom we owe very much for what we know about the Western Sudan in medieval times, has left us an account of the fine houses of the new wealthy class in the Sudan. El Bekri mentions houses built of stone and timber. This improved type of dwelling in the Western Sudan, possibly humble in the beginning, would no doubt continue as time went on to improve in architectural beauty with more and more Sudanese attaining wealth. When French archaeologists excavated the site of Kumbi, believed on fairly good evidence to be the capital of Old Ghana, they discovered the ruins of fine stone buildings of the type described by El Bekri. These stone buildings would undoubtedly be based upon North African models but adapted to conditions in the Western Sudan.

Islam in the Western Sudan
It was not only in material things that North African influences reached the Western Sudan. Islamic civilization and culture followed North African trade into the Western Sudan. In nearly all the big towns of the Sudan lived Moslems from North Africa. These were either merchants or religious teachers or men who combined both capacities. The Moslems brought into the Sudan their way of life and their methods of administra- tion. They were at all times a minority group, but they formed an influen-

tial body of people. We learn from El Bekri's accounts that the capital of Old Ghana had two sections – a Moslem and a pagan town. The former, with its mosques and stone houses, was the more imposing of the two and in all likelihood it was the Kumbi unearthed by French archaeologists. Moslems often held high offices in the various Sudanese kingdoms, and thus passed on their knowledge of administration to the native Sudanese. In Old Ghana the king's interpreters, the controller of his treasury and the majority of his ministers were chosen from among the Moslems.

The introduction of Islam into the Sudan influenced the lives of the Sudanese in several ways. Islam gave the Sudanese a new and wide outlook on the world, for all Moslems in medieval times looked upon themselves as common citizens of a world-wide state. The Sudanese Moslem who wanted to travel about in the Western Sudan outside his own tribe could count on the ready hospitality of fellow-Moslems. If he could afford to travel outside the Western Sudan altogether, he could still enjoy a warm Moslem welcome. The introduction of Islam also gave the Sudanese new moral standards. Islam forbade barbarous practices such as human sacrifices. It also introduced new ideas of law and justice as well as a new legal system in which justice was administered not by village elders guided by custom but by men trained to act as judges.

Writing and learning in general followed the introduction of Islam into the Western Sudan, as the result of the work of scholars and professional men from North Africa. We are told by Leo Africanus, who spent some time in the Western Sudan just after the end of the medieval period, that Timbuktu had 'great stores of judges, doctors, priests and other learned men' who were maintained on the king's account.

Leo goes on to mention books from North Africa 'which are sold for more money than merchandise'. Another Arab scholar, Es Sadi, gives a similar account of scholarship at another important place in the Western Sudan called Jenne. What was true of Timbuktu and Jenne might be true, more or less, of other towns in the Western Sudan. It appears that at least a small class of cultured Sudanese took a keen interest in general learning and even refined scholarship. In course of time there developed a famous centre of learning in Timbuktu around an institution called the Sankore Mosque, which attracted students and teachers from all parts of the Western Sudan and from abroad. It is believed that the Sankore Mosque was comparable to a medieval university.

Sudanese Moslems, like their fellow believers throughout the world, looked forward to a pilgrimage to Mecca as soon as they could afford it.

The kings of Mali, as we shall see in another chapter, made frequent pilgrimages to Mecca. The general pomp and free-spending which characterized the royal Mali visits to the Middle East greatly advertised the wealth of the Western Sudan. But more important still, Sudanese pilgrims had first-hand experience of Mediterranean culture and civilization and generally widened their outlook. The Emperor Mansa Musa of Mali, after a pilgrimage to Mecca in 1324, brought back with him to the Sudan a versatile Spanish Arab scholar and architect called Es-Saheli. No doubt Mansa Musa meant, through Es-Saheli, to put into practice some of the favourable impressions he had gained in the course of his pilgrimage. Es-Saheli is said to have built for Mansa Musa brick mosques in Gao and Timbuktu as well as a stone palace.

We need one word of caution about the various developments that followed the introduction of Islam into the Western Sudan. It would be rash and incorrect to suppose that Islam changed the general pattern of life in the Western Sudan completely: it did not. Many Sudanese only adopted Islam in a rather superficial way. Many more Sudanese did not care about Islam. Although they made use of Moslems and offered them privileged positions, the kings of Old Ghana themselves remained pagans. The Mossi to the south of the Western Sudan bravely and successfully defended paganism against the introduction of Islam. In nearly all parts of the Western Sudan the old and the new ways marched side by side as in fact they still do in many areas of Africa even today. However, although empires and kingdoms rose and fell in the Western Sudan, Islam remained as a new force in the vast area. Islam is today the religion of many peoples of the Western Sudan.

Eastern contacts and influences

The eastern corner of the Western Sudan, the Chad region and the area south-west of it, appear to have come under influences from the east, that is, possibly from the Nile valley. The channels and vehicles of eastern influences are not as clear as those from North Africa, as we have just seen. There is, however, some evidence in the form of common traditions of eastern origins worthy of discussion and examination. An interesting subject for examination in this respect is what is called the *Kisra Legend*. The Legend is common in Northern Nigeria, particularly from Wukari on the Benue to Idah and Busa on the Niger. The main point in the Legend is that an eastern prince called Kisra made his way into the Western Sudan where he founded a number of states. Traces of this tradition are also met with in Songhai.

Various attempts have been made to establish the Kisra Legend by connecting the name Kisra with words from Sudanese languages. For example, Kisra has been connected with the Hausa words *Sarki* or *Seraki* and the Busa word *ki-shira*. The whole position is by no means clear. However, it is interesting to note that traditions in various parts of Nigeria and the Chad region strongly assert that the ancestors of some Western Sudanese peoples came from the east. The tradition of a migration from the east led by a prince is strong in Borgu and Nupe. The Yorubas are almost certain that their ancestors came from the east. Moreover, there are said to be Kisra relics in a place called Karissen in the form of spears and a drum preserved to this day and believed by the local people to have belonged to Prince Kisra. What these relics are, we cannot say for certain, and we may never know. However, in the face of such popular traditions the possibility of a migration from the east to the Western Sudan cannot be easily dismissed.

Whether an eastern prince called Kisra did lead a migration to the Niger and Chad regions remains a mystery. What appears very probable is that small waves of immigrants entered the Western Sudan from the east in early or medieval times. There appears to have been some sort of link between the Nile valley and the eastern end of the Western Sudan. It is believed that when the ancient city of Meroë in the Nile valley (located in the present Republic of the Sudan) was destroyed in A.D. 350 by the king of Axum in Ethiopia, some members of the Meroë royal family moved south-west into Darfur, half-way between the River Nile and Lake Chad, where they established themselves as rulers. Archaeological findings seem to suggest that the influence of Meroë outside the Nile valley was strong in the area around Lake Chad, and that 'iron working, trade, ideas and people must have come from Meroë to influence societies of Negro Africa in many ways'.* Groups of nomadic people who were skilful craftsmen and known as the Zaghawa, moving westward from the Nile valley, entered various parts of the Western Sudan in early or medieval times. They appear to have left marks of their craftsmanship in parts of the Western Sudan. Today throughout Hausaland, in Northern Nigeria, there are castes of craftsmen known as *Zogoran* and *Zagurma*, names possibly derived from Zaghawa. It has been suggested that some of the domestic animals now common in Western Africa have come from Egypt and the Nile valley. The straight-backed and humped forms of the ox are believed to have reached Lake Chad and the Niger from eastern

* *History of Archaeology in Africa,* Report of a Conference held in July 1953 at the School of Oriental and African Studies, University of London, p. 39.

Africa; and so have the dog, the goat, the sheep and the domestic fowl, the last of which has not yet penetrated some remoter parts of the forest regions of Equatorial Africa. The main point is that in early and medieval times there was a link by some sort of route between the Nile valley and the Western Sudan, especially the area around Lake Chad. Small waves of migration seem to have gone on. Possibly the Kisra Legend is a shadowy recollection of one of these immigrant waves. Tradition of eastern origins is quite persistent in the region of Lake Chad. There are legends in Nupe that the followers of one Issa introduced weaving and the manufacture of cloth into that country. The early people of Borgu are said to have described themselves as the sons of Issa. An interesting point that may be raised in connection with influences from the east is the question of divine kingship. This is a common feature of political, social and religious life in the Western Sudan as well as in West Africa in general. It has been suggested that the institution of divine kingship spread out of the Nile valley into Africa. In many parts of Western Africa, as in ancient Egypt, the king occupied the position of a god. His state of health, it was believed, corresponded to the prosperity of the land as well as the general well-being of his people. The king was thus not allowed to grow too weak from old age and sickness. His reign might be limited to a definite number of years at the end of which, in early times, he was put to death; in later times a slave was killed in his place. There was a strong belief in life after death, and the king or the victim sacrificed in place of him met his end calmly in the faith that he was only passing into another life. Again in parts of West Africa, as in ancient Egypt, the king was protected from public gaze except on rare and special occasions. El Bekri has left an interesting description of royal burial in Old Ghana which conforms with divine worship and common practices in the remoter parts of Africa until quite recently. The Yorubas buried their dead in the Egyptian fashion of the crouching position. However, these developments are so old that it is quite difficult to make any positive statement concerning their origin. We cannot say for certain that divine kingship in West Africa originated from Egypt and the Nile valley. It is quite possible that certain aspects of divine kingship may have developed independently in different parts of Africa.

To conclude from all that has been said concerning the Kisra Legend and divine kingship on the main question of possible influences that entered the Western Sudan from the east, it may be pointed out that there is little that is very definite. However, this uncertainty does not necessarily destroy the possibility of contact between east and west with the Lake Chad area acting as the meeting ground. In about A.D. 1300, when King Sakora of Mali, returning home from a pilgrimage to Mecca by way of Axum (Aksum) in Ethiopia, was assassinated by the Danakil on the coast of Tajoura in Somalia, his body was carried to Bornu and thence to Mali. Some sort of route may have existed between east and west; but probably no significant trade developed along it. The details of traditions of eastern origins are obscure. It seems almost certain, however, that small groups of people entered the Western Sudan and other parts of Western Africa from the east. These immigrants influenced the pre-existing peoples with their cultures and ideas, and in the end there occurred a general fusion of cultures.

2 The peoples of the Western Sudan

The bulk of the population of the Western Sudan is Negro; but non-Negro elements from the north and north-east gradually penetrated the Sudanese grassland from early times and by the end of the medieval period they had settled permanently there. Arabs, Berbers and Tuareg all in early and medieval times made their way into the Western Sudan. Groups of nomadic pastoralists moving from the southern fringes of the Sahara into the savanna to graze and water their beasts periodically might decide in the end to settle down in the more favourable conditions of the Western Sudan. Intermarriage and consequent fusion between the immigrant 'Whites' and the Negro inhabitants of the Western Sudan followed. The Western Sudan is therefore not the home of the true Negro in the way that the West African forest belt is (Map 3).

An eminent writer of the history of the Western Sudan once attributed the political achievements of the Mandingo, Songhai and Hausa peoples of the Western Sudan to the infusion of White blood into Negro veins. We need not go as far as this, for the world of the mid-twentieth century is learning to be careful about such racial claims. All the same it is true that the contribution of the 'Whites' to the general culture and progress of the Western Sudan as a whole has been very considerable. They contributed to the foundation of some of the great states of the Western Sudan. For some six hundred years the Ghana empire is said to have been ruled by 'Whites'. Berbers played some part in the building of the empire of Songhai. Kanem and Bornu around Lake Chad came under very stimulating influences of non-Negro peoples. The Hausa-speaking peoples occupying the area stretching from the Niger-Benue confluence up to the desert south of Agades also came under Berber influence in medieval times. In many parts of the Western Sudan there gradually took place a mixture of Negro and White cultures and blood.

The Tuareg

Of all the non-Negro peoples who influenced the general development of the Western Sudan the Tuareg may be ranked among the most outstanding. This is not so much for the political contribution by the Tuareg as for their helping to keep open the culturally vital link between the Western Sudan and North Africa. It was the Tuareg who maintained the caravan routes across the desert into the Sudan. In medieval times the nomadic Tuareg inhabited the Central and Western Sahara. The Arabs called them Mulethemin, that is to say, the Veiled People, because of their habit of wearing the veil. In early and medieval times they entered parts of the Sudanese savanna whence they drove their beasts for pasture. They are a tall, slender, handsome and fair-skinned race. They are divided into several groups of tribes, the most important being the Sanhaja and the Lemtuna. The latter established themselves in the north-west corner of the Western Sudan with their capital at Audaghost.

The Tuareg were converted to Islam at an unknown period. The interesting thing about them is that it is the men and not the women who wear the veil. The men never part with the veil which they begin to wear from about the age of fifteen. The Tuareg remain veiled all the time, even inside their tents, even while eating and drinking. It is said that if a Targui* falls in battle, and his veil is swept off, his friends must veil his face again before they can decide who he is: without his veil he looks a complete stranger even before his closest associates. The Tuareg, unlike the other peoples of northern Africa, possess a non-Arabic script called T'ifinagh believed to be Phoenician in origin.

What really made the Tuareg important in the general development of the Western Sudan in medieval times was their maintenance of the caravan routes – the vital link between North Africa and the Sudan. The historical importance of the Tuareg cannot be over-emphasized. They were the camel-drivers of the Sahara and they controlled the main caravan routes – from Tripoli to Lake Chad, Tunis to Gao, Tlemcen to Timbuktu and from Fez to Audaghost. The Tuareg had a virtual monopoly of the real knowledge of these routes. They bred camels, cultivated the oases and dug and maintained wells at convenient points. They sometimes preyed upon the trans-Saharan trade, but they were wise enough not to do so to a degree that would ruin the traffic; for they realized how dependent they were upon the regular flow of trade.

In early medieval times the Tuareg appear to have had considerable power in the Western Sudan. In the ninth century they were able to

* Targui = singular of Tuareg.

dominate a number of Negro tribes from whom they exacted tribute. It was the Tuareg who founded Timbuktu and this gave the Western Sudan what was to become its greatest entrepôt and seat of learning. However, they were never sufficiently organized politically to establish a state or kingdom in the Western Sudan comparable to the medieval Negro kingdoms.

The Fulani

The Fulani or Fula, as they are sometimes called, are thought to belong to the 'White' population of the Western Sudan. They did not play any spectacular part in the political development of the Western Sudan in medieval times. They became important from the beginning of the nineteenth century when they conquered Hausaland and established the Fulani empire in what is today Northern Nigeria, and where they still remain the ruling aristocracy.

The Fulani are a shy pastoral race, rather non-Negroid in appearance. They have straight hair, a straight nose, thin lips, slight physique and light reddish-brown skin colour. Both men and women have a very graceful bearing. In medieval times their main homeland was in the Upper Senegal from where they gradually moved eastward, reaching Hausaland by the end of the thirteenth century. Today they live mostly in the Futa Jalon in the Republic of Guinea, Massina and in Northern Nigeria. They are of two main groups: the Fulani Bororo or Cattle Fulani, and the Fulani Gida or Town Fulani. The Bororo have tended to avoid mixture with the Negro populations among whom they dwell in a sort of symbiotic relationship and have preserved the purity of their blood. The Fulani Gida on the other hand have intermarried with the Negro Sudanese and have subsequently acquired negroid features.

The origins of the Fulani used to be considered a mystery. In fact enough is now known about their origins to dispel the Fulani as the 'mystery' people of West Africa. The theory that their ancestors were Jews who may have wandered into the Western Sudan in early times need not worry the student. Studies have shown that their origins are to be sought in West Africa and not in any alien and remote non-Negro elements. The Fulani language has been shown to be a Negro language related to the languages of the Serer and Wolof peoples of the Upper Senegal region. The original home of the Fulani, as we have seen, is the Senegal valley and the savanna region of the Futa Toro and just south of it.

The Fulani are believed to be the offspring of Berber fathers and

Tukulor mothers. The Tukulor are a Negro people of the Upper Senegal and akin to the Serer and the Wolof. The Tukulor state was a well-ordered one in which Berber herdsmen from the desert began to live side by side with the Tukulor of the fertile lands of the Upper Senegal. Cut off from their womenfolk the Berber herdsmen took Tukulor women as wives and thus began a process that finally resulted in their 'acculturation' to the Tukulor. Throughout human history any nomadic peoples settled among sedentary peoples have shared a similar fate. The Fulani Bororo and the Fulani Gida have common origins; their cultural differences stem from their attitudes to the local peoples among whom they found themselves living in the savanna of the Western Sudan.

The Fulani are generally Moslem and it is not difficult to explain this. The Tukulor state was politically powerful as early as about the seventh century A.D. The Tukulor appear at that time to have been independent of the Ghana empire. Following the example of their kings, the Tukulor became enthusiastic Moslems in the eleventh century; in fact they are said to have been the first Negro people to be converted to the Moslem faith in the Western Sudan. When the Fulani began to move out of the Tukulor state, gradually extending eastward, they carried the Moslem faith along with them. It may be pointed out, however, that many of the Fulani cared little about the new faith; some of them remained at best only nominal Moslems.

The Negro Sudanese
The Western Sudan is generally speaking not the home of the true Negro in the way that the forest belt to the south is. We see in this savanna of easy communication and movement a mixture of Negro and non-Negro peoples. It is certain, however, that the Negroes have inhabited the Western Sudan from pre-historic times. A Negroid skeleton discovered 250 miles north of Timbuktu is said to indicate that the inhabitants have not undergone ethnic change since Palaeolithic or Early Stone Age times. In historic times Negroes have always formed the basis of population in the Western Sudan. References were made to Blacks immediately south of the Sahara in Roman times. Negro peoples extended considerably farther north, occupying all of Fezzan where negroid physical traits are still quite noticeable. It is interesting to note that Negroes were expelled from the oasis of Kufra in the desert as recently as 1813. The Arabic term Bilad-as-Sudan, as we have already noted, means 'Land of the Negro'. Arabic scholars who wrote about the Western Sudan in medieval times were clear about who the inhabitants

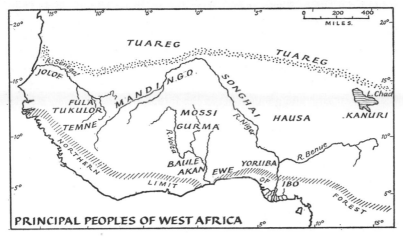

PRINCIPAL PEOPLES OF WEST AFRICA

Map 3

were: they were Negroes. The medieval kingdoms of Ghana, Mali and Songhai, whatever debt they owed to outsiders for their origins and development, were Negro or truly Sudanese in the sense that Negroes were their main peoples if not their actual founders.

Whatever movement of peoples may have gone on in the Western Sudan, the pattern of population does not seem to have changed much since medieval times. The Negro of the Sudan are split into linguistic rather than tribal groupings. Together with most other peoples of West Africa they speak a basic language classified as Sudanic. This may seem to point to a common heritage of the West African Negro in general.

The speakers of Sudanic languages in the savanna are divided into small divergent stocks, each occupying a compact territory stretching from the end of the desert to the margin of the forest to the south. In the extreme west along the Atlantic coast are peoples of distinct languages, probably suggesting an early entry and subsequent development of self-contained populations.

The Mande
Along the Senegal and the Gambia Rivers live the Woloff (Jolof), Serer and Tukulor. The region lying between the Senegal and the Niger is the main home of the Mandingo or more correctly the Mande-speaking peoples. The Mandingo constituted without any doubt the most influential elements in the Western Sudan in medieval times. They spread

around the Upper Niger, reaching as far south as latitude 9°N. They include such large tribes as the Dyula, Kassonke, Bambara, Jallonke, Malinke, Soninke and the Vei. These generally tall and slender people with fine features and fairly light complexion were the builders of the great medieval Sudanese kingdoms. They were the founders of a Sudanese civilization which penetrated to the south and no doubt influenced cultural and political life in the forest belt. Enterprising Mande traders in small numbers entered the forest for gold and kola and established small but influential colonies in many places. The goldfields of Asante, it is believed, formed one of the sources which made Old Ghana known to the Arabs as 'The land of gold'. It was Mande traders who conducted the traffic in gold. The Akan people of the Republic of Ghana still refer to travellers from the Sudanese savanna as the Wangara, most likely recalling the medieval Mande-traders from the gold-bearing region of Wangara, successfully controlled by Ghana, Mali and Songhai. A Bonduku tradition attributes the founding of Begho to the Mande. Begho lies on an old route leading from the Western Sudan into the southern forest. It is also believed that it was Mande groups who formed the nucleus of the Gonja state north of the Black Volta. It was Mande traders also who, in the late medieval period, pioneered the trade routes across northern Ghana and Borgu to Hausaland who first introduced Islam to Hausaland.

The Songhai
Along the Niger north of Busa and up to Gao on the great bend live the Songhai, builders of territorially the greatest medieval Sudanese empire. The Songhai are essentially Negroes but they have absorbed northern blood. In spite of the mixture with the Tuareg and Fula they have preserved their unity as a distinct people. They possess a single language and Islam is their religion. Their skin is coppery brown and never as dark as that of the inhabitants of the Guinea Coast.

The Mossi
In the hollow of the great bend of the Niger and stretching down to the edge of the southern forest live a large body of Negro peoples who speak the Gur or Voltaic group of languages. Among the most numerous in this group are the Mossi, a tenacious people with an interesting role in the history of the Western Sudan. The Mossi states possess a remarkable cohesion dating back to medieval times. Although the Mossi did not establish empires or kingdoms comparable to Ghana, Mali and

Songhai, they have for centuries remained closely knit. They not only beat off repeated attacks by their more enlightened neighbours to the north, but they also carried successful reprisal raids into Mali and Songhai territory. They sacked Timbuktu about 1333 and also raided Benka. From 1477 to 1483 the Upper Niger was subjected to severe Mossi attacks. During the same period Massina was at their mercy.

The Hausa
North of the Niger and the Benue, in the area stretching northward to the approaches of the desert, live the Hausa. The Hausa have since medieval times played an important part in the history of the eastern half of the Western Sudan. They established a number of states in Northern Nigeria. The influence of the Hausa as keen traders, shrewd business men and most skilful craftsmen is tremendous. In medieval times the Hausa lived in nearly all parts of the eastern half of the Western Sudan; in fact they were nearly as widespread as they are today. They penetrated various parts of the southern forest. Like the Mande, the Hausa lived in small colonies everywhere, displaying their wares, teaching their skills and winning converts to Islam. An important trade link between the Hausa states and the northern region of the Republic of Ghana dates back from the fourteenth century. Towns such as Salaga owe much to the presence of Hausa trading communities. Today Hausa is the most widely spoken African language in West Africa.

Strictly speaking there is no Hausa race, for Hausa is a linguistic term. There are Hausa-speaking peoples. Hausa is essentially a Hamitic language. It has been said that the Hausa originated from a mixture of diverse racial elements, one of the most important being the Tuareg, who had moved from the steppe-lands of the north into the rich agricultural areas around Lake Chad. Daura to the north-east of Katsina is believed to have been ruled by a long line of queens who were very probably of Berber origin. Hausa traditions lay strong emphasis on the origins of the Hausa-speaking peoples in the remote east. The Hausa, however, have essentially negroid features. They certainly have absorbed Negro blood like the other mixed negroid groups of the Western Sudan. The typical Hausa has been described as very black, like most of the Central Sudanese. He is essentially long-headed, and less muscular than the West Coast Negro, but is taller, having great length of leg.

The Chadic peoples
Bornu Province of Northern Nigeria brings us roughly to the limits of the

Western Sudan. Bornu and the area immediately around Lake Chad harboured mixed peoples in medieval times. The most important groups of people in Bornu today are the Kanembu and the Kanuri. There are also the Tedda and the Bulala. All these peoples claim non-Negro origins. Most of their traditions point to Berber and Arab ancestry. It appears certain, however, that in early times the Lake Chad region had a basic Negro population. The key to the early and medieval history of Bornu is to be found in its geographical position. As a well-watered region it was attractive to nomadic tribes from the desert. The well-known process of fusion between visiting nomads and the pre-existing peoples followed. This is the clue to the mixed populations in the region of Lake Chad. The region was originally inhabited by Negro tribes known as the So. They were organized on a clan system and they lacked adequate military co-operation. When nomadic tribes from the Sahara fell on Wadai just east of Lake Chad, the aboriginal tribes were unable to repel them. The invading nomads, who in all likelihood possessed superior military and political skill, soon over-ran the So and established themselves as rulers. There is an account in Kanem that the native population was overcome by a veiled tribe called the Saifi. The Saifi gradually dominated the So.

The picture we have before us around Lake Chad is one in which, at various intervals in early and medieval times, non-Negro peoples entered the region and by virtue of superior arms and skill they succeeded in imposing their rule upon the pre-existing Negro peoples. The Bornu region today has a mixed population ranging from strongly Hamitized groups to pure Negroes.

3 The medieval empires of the Western Sudan

Introduction

Three brief general observations may be made before entering upon a discussion of the fortunes of the Western Sudanese kingdoms or empires that flourished in the medieval era. The first observation concerns the territorial extent of the empires. The Western Sudanese empires never enjoyed the advantage of fixed boundaries. The open nature of the land in general made the limits of the empires quite fluid. Any attempt to show the boundaries and extent of the empires on historical maps may at best be regarded as a general guide. In his valuable *Atlas of African History*, J. D. Fage* represents the empires and kingdoms with circles, suggestive of balloons that could be inflated or deflated to the required size. The significance of this idea cannot be over-emphasized (Map 4, p. 41).

The second observation concerns the degree of authority exercised by the rulers of the empires. Obviously those territories and peoples nearer the centre of administration would be more closely controlled than those farther away. The strength of resistance of a conquered territory would determine its relationship with the centre of authority. If the conquered people became rebellious and ably held their own against a punitive expedition sent into their territory, they might well succeed and regain their independence to all intents and purposes. The subjection of territories farther away would probably not go beyond the exaction of of tribute for a while. Those territories on the fringes of the empire may only have succumbed to a raiding expedition that pillaged districts, collected booty, departed and made an end of the whole affair. In short, it is important to realise that while some areas of the empires were closely administered, others would carry on with the normal course of

* Edward Arnold, 1958.

life barely aware of the ruling hand of the emperor. In some conquered territories the old rulers would become the vassals of the emperor; in others governors might be sent out by the emperor, perhaps his own relatives or friends, or able generals and captains he wished to reward for good services rendered. The whole organization was bound to become strained and fairly loose as the empire kept on expanding or became exhausted with time and care.

The last point to consider is the nature of the general progress and culture attained by the peoples of the empires – both governors and governed. The king-emperors, according to the various accounts that have come down to us, maintained elaborate courts. The accounts by both visitors and scholars glow with scenes of splendour and high cultural attainments. Kumbi, Jenne, Gao, Timbuktu, Kano, Njimi were all considerably impressive places. However, it is possible for the student to exaggerate the general state of affairs in the empires. The student would do well to guard against overestimation. Whole tribes, including those of the emperors, might continue for centuries to live peaceful and simple lives scarcely influenced by the wealth and culture of the big towns. It must always be kept in mind that the medieval Sudanese, whether Negro or 'White', were ordinary men and women who lived as befitted their time and place. Some realism is required to understand the history of the medieval empires of the Western Sudan.

Ghana

Origins of the kingdom
The origins of Old Ghana remain obscure. The principal sources of our information, namely the records left by Arabic scholars, do not throw sufficient light on the question of Ghana's origins. The Arabic scholars all wrote about Ghana when the kingdom had already entered its great period of prosperity. We are even left in some doubt concerning the actual name by which the kingdom as a whole or its capital town was known. Several of the Arabic scholars, for example Al Fazari, Al-Kwarizmi and Yakoubi, give the name of the land and of the kingdom as Ghana. However, El Bekri adds that 'Ghana is also the title given to their kings; the name of the region is Aukar'. He mentions also that 'the town in which the king lives bears the name El Ghaba'. The *Tarik el Fettach,* the work of a Sudanese scholar, written in the seventeenth century, alone gives the name of the capital town of the kingdom of Ghana as Kumbi, ruins of which have been uncovered by French archaeologists.

The question of who founded the kingdom of Ghana is equally obscure. Some historians maintain that Ghana was founded by 'Whites', but this is a theory about which other historians differ. The mention of White founders was first made in the *Tarik el Fettach*. It may be noted that the author of the *Fettach*, Mahmoud Kati, a native Sudanese of mixed descent, was by no means certain about this assertion. Let Kati speak for himself: 'People do not agree', he wrote, 'to the tribe to which these (White) princes belonged; ... they may have been Sanhaja ... God knows it better than anyone ... It is not possible nowadays for historians without fear of contradiction to agree on this subject'. On the other hand it is important to note that the Arabic writers – Yakoubi in the ninth century A.D., Masudi and Ibn Hawqal in the tenth century; and Al Birouni and El Bekri in the eleventh century – all described the people of Ghana as Negro. As we saw in the last chapter, the Negroes of the Western Sudan are not all of dark skin like most inhabitants of the West African forest. Could it be that some fair-skinned Negro Sudanese were mistaken for 'Whites'? Even in the West African forest one sometimes sees surprisingly fair-skinned Negroes. Whole villages east of the Lower Volta in the Republic of Ghana are inhabited by conspicuously fair-skinned people. Dagomba tradition attributes the founding of that state to one Tahajiye, a Negro of light complexion. His name really means *red hunter*.

Some scholars who have devoted themselves to the study of races in the Western Sudan are agreed that it was Negroes of the Mande sub-family and not some unidentified White group as is sometimes alleged, who formed the core of the old empire of Ghana. What shall we say about the founders of Ghana then? It is most likely that the founders of Old Ghana were Mande-speaking Negroes, probably of light skin colour. However, it may also be that the unidentified 'Whites' were some of the non-Negro elements from the north who found their way into the Western Sudan in early times. What appears certain, however, is that the bulk of the people of Old Ghana were Negro – a branch of the Mande-speakers called the Soninke. Ghana as a matter of fact did not reach its most prosperous period under the alleged 'White' rulers but under the Soninke.

The founding of Ghana is usually placed in the second or third century A.D. This is based upon a tradition recorded by Es Sadi in his work the *Tarik el Sudan* (History of the Sudan). The tradition says that the kingdom of Ghana existed before Hejira, that is, the year A.D. 622, which is really the first year of the Mohammedan era. Before that date, according to Es

B

Sadi, twenty-two White kings had reigned in Ghana. Another twenty-two White kings reigned after Hejira, so we have a dynasty of forty-four kings of White race neatly divided by Hejira. Perhaps all that it means is that the dynasty and Ghana itself existed before Hejira. The third or probably the fourth century, however, appears to be a reasonable period to date the founding or the coming into prominence of Ghana in the Western Sudan. Ghana owed its rise to prominence, if not its origins, to the growth of the trans-Saharan trade. This trade appears in all likelihood to have assumed considerable importance only after the camel had come into use as the 'ship of the desert', and this was not until early in the Christian era. The introduction of the camel as a matter of fact revolutionized the entire trans-Saharan trade and so created the situation that promoted the growth of the Sudanese kingdoms of which Ghana was the first.

We may then say that Ghana began to emerge as a prominent state or kingdom in the Western Sudan early in the Christian era. Although little is known for certain about the actual origins of Ghana, the circumstances of its rise to fame and influence can be fairly well assessed from certain known facts about the Western Sudan in the Middle Ages. Ghana lay between the Sahara and the southern forest. It was near the great bend of the Niger. Although where Kumbi, the capital of Ghana, stood is today dry and swallowed up by the desert, it was not so in early and medieval times. Some degree of desiccation has gone on in the region over the centuries. The early records speak of rich lands around Ghana. 'Around the town are wells of sweet water from which they drink and near which they grow vegetables'. El Bekri, who wrote this, then gave the name of the king's town as El Ghaba, and explained its meaning as 'the forest'. Ghana then, the evidence shows, stood in a fairly fertile region. South of Ghana lay the rich gold-bearing region of Wangara, now identified as the present Bambuk region. Here gold was won by Negroes who bartered it for salt and other goods from outside. It is interesting to note that in the same region today each year some 70,000 to 100,000 Africans are said to pan gold during the dry season, in comformity with traditional techniques and quasi-religious rites.

News of Sudanese gold may have reached North Africa in early times. This may have given the old trans-Saharan trade a great boost to which Ghana owed its rise to fame if not its actual origin. The gold-bearing region of Wangara was never within real Ghana territory, but Ghana obtained control of the gold trade. The earliest Arabic records about Ghana connected her with gold. El Fazzari about A.D. 800 mentioned among a list of African countries 'the territory of Ghana, the land of gold'.

Yakoubi wrote in A.D. 872 'The king of Ghana is a great king. In his territory are gold mines and he has under his domination a great number of kingdoms'. Then Hawqal about 977, writing about Audaghost, made the reference that 'the kings of this town (Audaghost) have relations with the king of Ghana who is the richest on earth because of his gold'. Al Masudi, the Arabic geographer who died in 956, left a most interesting description of the gold trade of Ghana. He wrote:

'The Kingdom of Ghana is of great importance, and it adjoins the land of the gold mines. Great peoples of the Sudan live there. They have traced a boundary which no one who sets out to them passes. When the merchants reach this country, they place their wares and cloth on it and then depart, and so the people of the Sudan come, bearing gold, which they leave beside the merchandise and then [themselves] depart. The owners of the merchandise then return and if they are satisfied with what they have found, they take it. If not they go away again, and the people of the Sudan return and add to the price until the bargain is concluded. All the gold which the merchants obtain is minted in the town of Sijilmasa ... Under the supreme rule of the king of Ghana, there are a number of lesser rulers, and in all their kingdoms gold is visible on the ground and people extract it and set it like curds'. When the outside world first heard of Ghana it was in connection with gold. Ghana exploited its position lying between producers of two important commodities: gold-bearing Wangara and the salt mines of the desert. Salt was a rare luxury in the Western Sudan. To the north of Ghana and deep in the Sahara Desert lay the salt mines of Taghaza. Traders from North Africa stopped at Taghaza where they loaded salt on the back of camels. The cargo of salt was taken to Ghana where it was bartered for gold. The trade in gold and salt was a highly profitable one for both North African merchants and Sudanese middlemen. One Arabic writer even tells us that salt was worth its own weight in gold. The merchants from North Africa never had access to the gold mines: the mining locations were kept a secret by Ghana which controlled the whole gold traffic.

It may then be said that Ghana owed its rise to fame and power in the Western Sudan to the fact that it was fairly easily accessible from the north by carefully chosen caravan routes. It was the centre of the trans-Saharan trade, placed as it was between producers of two valuable commodities: gold and salt. In addition to salt, Ghana received North African articles of trade like cloth, beads, glass and dried dates. Ceuta in Morocco became a bead-manufacturing centre to meet the demand from the Sudan. Besides gold, Ghana offered ostrich feathers, and later slaves.

Social and economic life in Ghana

The unearthed ruins of Kumbi, the capital of Ghana, cover a square mile and suggest a fairly large medieval urban settlement; but the ruins apparently represent the Moslem section of the capital. The capital was divided into a Moslem section and a pagan section. The pagan section, the actual seat of government and where the king lived, appears to have been only a large village. Its houses for the most part were of mud walls and thatch roofs, a type of building that is still very common in rural Africa. Paganism was the rule rather than the exception in Ghana. The king-emperor was himself a pagan, although he tolerated and even trusted Moslems.

The king of Ghana often gave audience to his people to listen to their complaints and to give them justice. When he did this he sat in a pavilion around which stood his horses richly adorned in cloth of gold. Beside the king stood pages holding shields and gold-mounted swords. On his right sat the sons of the governors and princes of the empire splendidly dressed. The beginning of the royal session was announced by the beating of a drum which the people of Ghana called *deba*. There is a kind of drum used in the Western Sudan still known by the name deba.

The people of Ghana were pagans who worshipped idols. On the death of the king they erected a special hut made of wood within which they made the royal grave. The corpse was put on a bed and placed in the burial edifice. Near the dead body were placed his ornaments, weapons and dishes and cups he had used for his food and drink. Several of the king's cooks and drink makers were shut up with the body in the hut. Then the people covered the entire edifice with mats and finally threw earth over it until a big mound was formed. For some time afterwards victims were sacrificed to the dead king, and drinks were offered to the dead.

Trade was extremely important to the life of Ghana. The relation between Ghana's rise to fame and the trans-Saharan trade has already been mentioned. The revenue of the kingdom was derived, to a great extent, from taxes levied on trade. The king collected a special tax of one gold dinar on each standard load of salt coming into his kingdom and twice as much on salt leaving the kingdom for places farther south; to Wangara, for example. There was so much gold in circulation that a law had to be passed giving all nuggets to the king and leaving the gold dust for the people. The control of the taxation machinery was entrusted to Moslems.

There is no doubt that a fair number of the native Soninke of Ghana became wealthy through the trans-Saharan trade. However, the great majority of the people of Ghana were ordinary peasants. Their daily routine of life would probably conform more or less to that of rural populations in general in many parts of Africa a hundred or so years ago. Naturally the main pre-occupation of the country people was farming, the general level of which is not easy to determine. In some parts of the empire, farming might have been at about subsistence level employing simple methods. Today, while many of the Western Sudanese peoples only scratch the soil with light hoes and dibble in their seed to secure a quick crop, others such as the Hausa, the Bambara and Malinke practise deep hoeing and ridge cultivation and sometimes even irrigation. How far back this improved type of cultivation goes into the history of the Western Sudan is difficult to say. It is, however, an interesting development in which the Soninke of Ghana might well have shared even in medieval times.

The expansion and fall of Ghana
Ghana reached its peak from about the middle of the eight century to the middle of the eleventh. It is said that about A.D. 770 the last 'White' king of Ghana was assassinated by the Soninke, and the Soninke chief of Wagadu, called Kaza-Maghan Sisse, became emperor of Ghana. Under Kaza-Maghan, Ghana entered a remarkable period of prosperity. When Arab merchants first entered the Western Sudan during the eighth century the Negro king of Ghana was the most powerful ruler in the Western Sudan. His authority extended over a wide area. By the middle of the ninth century the empire had reached its peak territorially. It included the greater part of Hodh and Tagant as well as Aukar and Bagara. To the east it was bounded by the Niger and to the west by the Senegal and the Baule.

The rapid expansion of Ghana in the eighth and ninth centuries seems to have been the result of a desire to get as much as possible out of the trans-Saharan trade which was beginning to assume great proportions after the Arabs had overrun the Western part of North Africa to which they gave the name Maghreb. Arab traders then began to reach the Western Sudan. The territorial expansion of Ghana probably took the form of an armed conquest. 'The king of Ghana', El Bekri recorded, 'can raise 200,000 warriors, 40,000 of them being armed with bows and arrows'. The king also possessed some cavalry, but the horses were small in size. The mention of the horse is an interesting clue to the expansion not only of Ghana with which we are immediately concerned, but also of the succeeding Sudanese kingdoms. The possession of the horse gave the armies of the Sudanese states mobility and a quick striking-force which greatly facilitated the extension of territorial power. The horse was important as a political and military instrument for it helped to concentrate military force at short notice and made possible rapid communication of orders from capital to province. Ghana in her expansion no doubt exploited these political and military advantages of cavalry. Displays of horse-riding on ceremonial occasions that go on throughout the Western Sudan today may well be taken as the symbol of what used to be the key to political and military power in the region.

The control which Ghana had in the Western Sudan came under threat early in the ninth century. Tilutane, a Berber chief of the Lemtuna tribe, putting himself at the head of a large army, began to bring the Berber tribes of the Western Sahara together in a sort of confederacy. His followers in Hodh and Tagant began to raid the neighbouring Negro tribes, including some under the suzerainty of Ghana. Tilutane turned the Lemtuna capital of Audaghost into a serious rival of Ghana. Audaghost, which was about fifteen days' march to the west from Ghana, was a very populous town. It had attracted a large number of Arab merchants who were doing prosperous business there. The Soninke of Ghana, aware of the challenge that Audaghost offered their own capital commercially and politically, waylaid and attacked caravans entering Audaghost from the north. The Berbers of Audoghost retaliated by engaging themselves in subversion against Ghana among her vassal chiefs. The Soninke gained the upper land by wrenching back from the Berbers districts that the latter had gained from Ghana. In A.D. 990 the town of Audaghost became tributary to Ghana.

A serious turn of events occurred in A.D. 1020 when the various Berber tribes of the Western Sahara, the Lemtuna, Jedala and Mesufa, united in a confederacy, the veiled purpose of which was to overthrow the supremacy of Ghana in the Western Sudan. Their head was a chief called Tarsina, recently converted to Islam. Tarsina made a pilgrimage to Mecca after which he began to wage a *jihad* or Moslem holy war on the neighbouring Negro peoples. After Tarsina had been killed in the course of this *jihad* his work fell on the shoulders of his son-in-law, Yahia Ibn Ibrahin. Like his father-in-law, Yahia made a pilgrimage to Mecca. On his return home through Sijilmasa he obtained the services of a Moslem theologian by name Abdula Ibn Yacin, who would instruct his people in the true Islamic faith. Ibn Yacin's work of reform among Yahia's easy-going Jedala subjects proved too much for them and in the end the theologian was chased out of the tribe.

The Almoravids

Ibn Yacin with a few faithful followers took shelter on an obscure islet in a neighbouring river. Yacin soon mustered about a thousand fanatical converts from among the neighbouring people. He named these *Morabethan*, who became subsequently known in the history of the Western Sudan as the Almoravids. They adopted a reformed Islamic faith of a most militant character. The Almoravids started off a *jihad* to compel the acceptance of their reformed faith. Their religious zeal was greatly reinforced by economic and political considerations. When Yacin denounced looting, his followers took offence. He then adopted a tyrannical attitude and in the end had to flee from the angry Almoravids. Yacin succeeded in reaching Sijilmasa in the north, where he won over a fresh horde of followers. Returning with these to the south, he began to master the tribes of the Western Sahara.

In 1054 the Almoravids captured Audaghost and put many of the inhabitants to the sword. When in 1059 Yacin was killed, Abu Bakr assumed control of the Almoravid movement. He continued Yacin's *jihad* farther north but had to hurry back to the Western Sudan on hearing that a quarrel had broken out in the section of the Almoravids in the south. Once he was back in the Sudan Abu Bakr soon restored order. However, he decided to find a distracting engagement for his unruly followers. He turned them against the Soninke of Ghana under their aged king Bassi. Thus the fate of Ghana became involved in the ungovernable behaviour of the fanatic Almoravids. In 1076 the Almoravids sacked Ghana (Kumbi) which was forced to pay tribute to Abu Bakr and a poll tax was imposed on the pagan population of the capital.

What was the impact of the Almoravid invasion on the Ghana empire? According to an old Arabic record the kingdom of Ghana declined into utter weakness after the invasion. The Tuareg who lived just to the north of Ghana began to pillage the territories of the empire, and compelled many to accept Islam. The empire began to disintegrate.

The Almoravid invasion was a big blow to the prestige and position of Ghana in the Western Sudan. However, 1076 did by no means see the end of Ghana, nor of her prosperity. But the Negro dynasty of Ghana was superseded by a Moslem Berber one. A second period of prosperity for Ghana began, and there was renewed commercial activity. It is thought that the fine stone houses and extensive Moslem cemeteries revealed by the excavation of the ruins of Kumbi date from this period of recovery which lasted for more than a century.

On the death of Abu Bakr in 1087 the influence of the Almoravids in the

Western Sudan vanished quite suddenly, but in spite of its recovery Ghana was politically never its old self again. The authority of the Soninke kings of Ghana was greatly reduced. Many parts of the empire regained their independence. In 1203 Sumanguru, king of a small but strong state called Kanianga, sent a successful expedition against the capital of Ghana. It appears that Sumanguru 'killed the goose that laid the golden eggs' by imposing too heavy taxation on the commerce of the old capital. The annoyed and frustrated traders left Kumbi in 1224 to settle in Walata, about a hundred miles to the north. In 1235 Sundiata, ruler of the growing kingdom of Mali, killed Sumanguru and over-powered his people, the Susu. In 1240 Sundiata occupied what still remained of Ghana. And so passed away Ghana after nearly a thousand years of influence and supremacy in the Western Sudan. From 1240 Ghana faded out very quickly. It is significant that the intelligent and critical Moslem traveller, Ibn Batuta, who visited the Western Sudan in 1353, made no mention whatsoever of Ghana in his accounts. Probably Ghana was no more; even its memory was temporarily gone.

Mali

Early history

Ghana's place of influence and power in the Western Sudan was taken over by Mali. A little more is known for certain about the history of Mali than of Ghana. The kings of Mali were generally staunch Moslems who made pilgrimages to Mecca. Records of their visits to the Mediterranean lands have made it possible to date fairly accurately important events in the history of Mali. Fortunately also, the great traveller Ibn Batuta, who visited Mali in the middle of the fourteenth century when the empire was at its zenith, has left a full and most interesting account of events connected with various aspects of life in Mali. Moreover, while the active history of Ghana covers a thousand years, that of Mali covers only about two hundred years of a later period and dominated by most active and sometimes picturesque rulers. However, this is not to say that we know all that we would wish to know about Mali.

The ruling people of Mali were Mandingoes who were closely related to the Soninke of Ghana. The territories that became the centre of the kingdom of Mali were obscure dependencies of Ghana from the eleventh century or possibly a little earlier.

One of the early kings of Mali called *Bermandana* was converted to Islam at the time of the Almoravid movement. He made a pilgrimage to

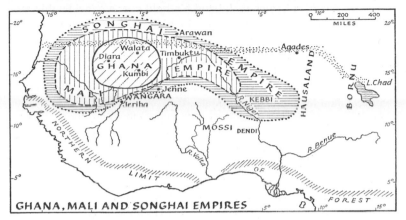

GHANA, MALI AND SONGHAI EMPIRES

Map 4

Mecca, and several of his successors followed the practice. The real founder of Mali as Ghana's successor in the Western Sudan was Sundiata, popularly known under his other name *Mari Djata.* The name *Djata,* which means 'a lion', testifies to the courage and masterfulness of Sundiata.

Sumanguru, the Susu king who had attacked Kumbi, capital of Ghana, in 1203, later turned his arms on Mali. Success seems not only to have attended his expedition but also to have turned his head, for he is said to have put to death eleven out of twelve Mali royal brothers who fell into his hands. Sundiata, a young cripple, was the only one whose life Sumanguru had spared either out of sympathy or spite.* Sumanguru's show of mercy to the cripple, whatever motive lay behind it, was to prove a turning point in the history not only of Mali but of the Western Sudan in general. Sundiata somehow became cured of his deformity. He quickly put himself at the head of a band of hunters with whose support he soon gained control over the kingdom of Mali. Although at first unpopular, Sundiata eventually won the respect and confidence of his people by embarking upon a career of conquest. First he conquered Wangara and added to his army in the process. Then he attacked the small kingdom of Labe in the Futa Jalon, adding further to his military strength. He then turned eastward, crossed the Niger and defeated Bambara, a tribe of fierce pagans.

* No comprehensive account from one source on Sundiata has come down to us. What is presented here is pieced together out of various sources largely based upon tradition.

By 1234 Sundiata had consolidated his hold over a considerable area and he now returned home to Mali in triumph. Sumanguru naturally viewed with alarm the strong position in which Sundiata now stood and determined to destroy Mali before it was too late. In 1235 Samanguru made an attack on Mali but was killed by Sundiata at Kirina. The Susu kingdom was then absorbed into Mali. Everything had steadily been on the ascendant for Sundiata and Mali.

Kumbi had by this time already fallen into obscurity. Its trading inhabitants, mainly Arabs, under their emir or leader, had withdrawn to Walata in 1224. In 1240 Sundiata attacked Kumbi and finally destroyed the former dominant power of the Western Sudan. After this victory Sundiata moved the capital of Mali from Jeriba to Niani. Sundiata never went out on a conquering expedition again; he left further conquests to his captains. Mali soon obtained control over the goldfields of Wangara and thus gained access to what seemed an inexhaustible source of wealth. When Sundiata died about 1255, after twenty-five years of a most exciting reign, Mali already controlled a large area of the Western Sudan. Mali's power extended far into the desert.

Mansa Musa

Sundiata was succeeded by Mansa Ule. Ule reigned till about 1270, but little is known about his achievements. For some twenty-five years after the death of Ule there was a rapid succession of kings, suggestive of a troubled period in the history of Mali. The situation was saved by a usurper called Sakora. It is not clear when and how Sakora seized the Mali stool; but he gave a good account of himself. He embarked upon further conquests for Mali. He subdued Gao, capital of the kingdom of Songhai. In about 1300 he made a pilgrimage to Mecca and died while returning home by way of eastern Africa.

It was left to Mansa Musa, the grandson of Sundiata's brother, Abu Bakr, who became king of Mali about 1307, finally to establish the Mali empire and to spread its fame abroad. Mali attained the peak of its territorial expansion under Mansa Musa. However, Mansa Musa's real claim to a place of distinction in the history of Mali lies not so much in this territorial expansion as in the fact that he won foreign recognition for his kingdom. This recognition he achieved largely by the great splendour that attended his pilgrimage to Mecca in 1324. He travelled through Walata and proceeded to Tuat in the desert. The route he followed after Tuat is not clear. We are told that Mansa Musa was accompanied on this pilgrimage by 60,000 attendants, but this appears unlikely considering the difficult problems of a long march across the desert. In any case, Mansa Musa took with him plenty of gold which he gave out lavishly to charity in Cairo and Mecca. So free did Mansa Musa prove with his gifts that he ran out of funds in the end and had to raise a loan before he could return home to the Sudan. Musa was shown great respect at all the places he visited in the Middle East. The various accounts of his pilgrimage leave no impression whatsoever that the Mali emperor suffered from any form of racial prejudice. A man called El-Omari recalls that on visiting Cairo twelve years after Mansa Musa had been there, he found many people still singing the praises of the Mali emperor.

Mansa Musa returned to the Sudan by the eastern caravan route through Ghadames. On his return journey Musa is said to have stopped at Gao to receive the submission of the town and to have taken with him to Mali as hostages two Songhai princes, Ali Kolen and Suleyman Nar.

Two interesting personages from North Africa accompanied Mansa Musa back to the Sudan. The first was a merchant of Alexandria who had come to Musa's aid when he ran short of money. This man died at Timbuktu before he could recover the loan. However, the fair-minded Musa later repaid the loan in full to the merchant's heirs. The second person was Es-Saheli, a Spanish Arab poet who was also an architect. Es-Saheli built brick mosques in Gao and Timbuktu. He also built a stone palace for Mansa in Timbuktu.

Mansa Musa died in 1332, leaving behind an enormous empire, the fame of which he had done so well to spread abroad. The Mali empire in 1332 extended from the Atlantic coast to Songhai far down the Niger bend to the east. The famous copper town of Takeda came under Mali control. To the south Mali territory stretched as far as the edge of the forests. This truly was 'remarkable both for its extent and its wealth, and a striking example of the capacity of the Negro for political organization'* Mansa Musa improved trade in his kingdom by establishing friendly relations with outside states such as Egypt and Arabia. He also cultivated the friendship of the Sultan of Fez.

For some fifty years after Mansa Musa's death his own fame as well as that of Mali continued to echo abroad. In 1339 Mali appeared on a new map of the world represented in the form of a royal figure placed in the Southern Sahara with the inscription *Rex Malley*. Another map of the world in 1367 showed a road leading from North Africa through the Atlas Mountains into the Western Sudan, with the following explanatory note:

* E. W. Bovill, *The Golden Trade of the Moors,* Oxford University Press, 1958, p. 90.

'Through which passes the merchandise from the kingdom of Mali'. Eight years later there appeared a third map of the world showing in the region south of the Sahara a richly attired monarch displaying ornaments of gold in his hand. The picture carried the following inscription: 'This Negro Lord is called Mansa Mali, Lord of the Negroes of the Guinea. So abundant is the gold which is found in his country that he is the richest and most noble king in all the land'.

Mansa Musa was succeeded by his son Maghan, who died after only four years' reign. Then a brother of Mansa Musa called Mansa Suleyman became king of Mali and reigned for twenty-four years. It was during Suleyman's reign that the famous traveller Ibn Batuta visited the kingdom of Mali (1353). Ibn Batuta has left an interesting and most valuable account of the things he saw in Mali. It is not possible here to make even a brief summary of Ibn Batuta's observations. It may only be pointed out that his final impressions were most favourable. He had fallen ill soon after reaching the Western Sudan, and probably becoming exasperated and ill-tempered, Batuta started with some rather unkind words about the Negroes. However, when he came to know the people better after he had recovered from his illness, he became full of admiration for the things he saw in Mali. He then began to talk fondly of the great learning of both native and foreign scholars he found in Mali. He praised the skill of a physician who attended him when he became ill. But what impressed Batuta most of all was the security of travelling about in Mali as well as the general sense of justice of the people. He wrote:

'The Negroes possess some admirable qualities. They are seldom unjust and have a greater abhorrence of injustice than any other people. Their sultan shows no mercy to anyone who is guilty of the least act of offence. There is complete security in their country. Neither traveller nor inhabitant in it has anything to fear from robbers or men of violence. They do not confiscate the property of any White man who dies in their country. On the contrary, they give it into the charge of some trustworthy person among the Whites, until the rightful heir takes possession of it'

Years of difficulties and decline
After the death of Mansa Suleyman the great days of Mali began quickly to pass away. Suleyman was succeeded by Mansa Djata, a tyrant whose twenty-four years' reign brought the empire no good. He spent money recklessly. He is said to have sold some state jewels including a precious collection of rare gold nuggets. He died of sleeping sickness, probably unmourned by his subjects. The end of the glory of Mali was not far away.

There had been gloomy signs even shortly after the death of the great Mansa Musa. About 1335 the Songhai had begun to fight to free themselves from Mali domination. The two Songhai princes, Ali Kolen and Nar, whom Mansa Musa had taken away from Gao as hostages, escaped from the Mali court and succeeded in making their way back home. They raised a Songhai army against the Mandingo soldiers who had been stationed in Songhai territory by Mansa Musa, and expelled them. Gao became free and Ali Kolen was proclaimed king of Songhai. Two years earlier, about 1333, the Mossi, living to the south of the Sudanese savanna along the River Volta, had sacked Timbuktu which was then under Mali control. In the 1380s a minister of the Mali court, later known as Musa II, attempted a revival of the Mali army with a view to arresting the general decline of Mali's position in the Sudan. He defeated the copper centre of Takeda which had lately declared itself independent of Mali. However, the movement for revival was short-lived. There were further troubles at the Mall court. King Magan II was assassinated and chaos followed. The progressive decline of Mali now seemed beyond recall. About the year 1400 the Mossi made another destructive raid into Mali territory. In c.1433, Akil, a Tuareg chief, captured Walata and Timbuktu. In 1468 Sonni Ali, king of Songhai, began to overrun Mali altogether. Mali soon counted for little in the Western Sudan.

4 The Songhai empire

Early history

During the course of the fifteenth century Mali was overshadowed by Songhai which now became the leading kingdom in the Western Sudan. Songhai eventually built the largest empire ever in the Sudan. The Songhai empire covered the territories previously held by Ghana and Mali, and more besides. However, the early history of Songhai, like that of Ghana and Mali, is rather obscure. The original home of the Songhai people was Dendi, along the Niger roughly half-way between the great bend of the river in the north and its confluence with the Benue. The Songhai were of two mutually hostile clans, the *Sorko* and the *Gabibi*. The former were mainly fisher-folk and the latter agricultural people. After a long history of conflicts between the two groups, the Sorko in the end dominated the Gabibi.

In the ninth century the Songhai were conquered by nomadic Tuareg of the branch called the Lemta from the north, under their leader Za Aliamen. The Lemta established themselves in the old Songhai capital of Kukia and Za Aliamen became the first of a long line of Berber kings of Songhai. Under pressure from the Lemta the Sorko section of the Songhai retreated northward along the Niger and set up an independent kingdom at Gao on the great bend. The Lemta followed the Sorko up the river and captured Gao in about A.D. 890. The Sorko, who were determined to remain independent, retreated farther north and finally settled down around Lake Debo after a sharp conflict with the Soninke.

Early in the eleventh century King Za Kossoi of the Berber-Songhai kingdom in Dendi removed his capital from Kukia to Gao. Za Kossoi soon afterwards became a Moslem. It seems that Za Kossoi decided to move the Songhai capital to Gao mainly for economic reasons. At the beginning of the eleventh century Gao had already become prosperous through the trans-Saharan trade. It had attracted a considerable number of Moslem traders from North Africa. We are told that Gao, like Kumbi of Ghana, had two sections: one pagan, the other Moslem.

The two Songhai princes who had been carried away from Gao by Mansa Musa as hostages eventually escaped. Ali Kolen was proclaimed king of Songhai and he began to drive out the Mali soldiers whom Mansa Musa had stationed in Songhai territory. This was a turning point in the history of Songhai. On becoming king, Ali Kolen took the title of Sonni and founded a new dynasty in Songhai. We know very little of Ali Kolen's achievements as king and of those of his sixteen successors of the Sonni dynasty. However, it seems that for over a hundred years the Songhai kings struggled to remain independent of Mali. There was practically no attempt during this obscure period to gain territories for the kingdom of Songhai. The task of empire-building through force of arms was left to Sonni Ali, one of the greatest names in the history of the Western Sudan.

Sonni Ali

Sonni Ali became king of Songhai in 1464. He was a soldier king. He announced his military career by a campaign against the Tuareg who had taken possession of Timbuktu from Mali control in c.1434. At first the Tuareg did not disturb the local government of the town; they left the governor or Koi of Timbuktu, a man called Naddi, to carry on with the day to day administration. On Naddi's death, shortly before Sonni Ali became king of Songhai, the affairs of Timbuktu were thrown into confusion. Akil, the leader of the Tuareg, would not deal fairly with the new Koi, Omar. Akil refused Omar, as Koi, the usual share of a third of the taxes collected in Timbuktu. Omar sent to Sonni Ali, asking for his help against the Tuareg and promising to deliver the town to the Songhai king. Ali had always borne the Tuareg and foreigners in the Western Sudan in general a great hatred and he quickly seized the opportunity to strike at his foes.

As Sonni Ali and his Songhai army marched towards Timbuktu, Akil and many of the prominent men in the town, including some scholars, took fright and fled to Walata. Omar also fled. Ali took Timbuktu in 1468 after sacking it and burning down some of its main buildings. For three years he ruled the town with an iron hand, openly showing hostiity to the foreigners and learned men who had remained behind. Although a Moslem, at least in name, Ali showed very little respect to the Islamic faith.

Sonni Ali's reign of thirty years was one long period of military service and glory. After mastering Timbuktu he marched south on Jenne.

Founded about 1250 by the Soninke, Jenne had developed fast as a flourishing commercial town as well as a centre of learning. After a long siege which is said to have lasted seven years, Jenne fell to Ali in about 1473. Ali showed very remarkable leniency to the people of Jenne. He now began to plan an attack on Walata both to punish Akil and the Tuareg who had fled there from Timbuktu and also to add the important town to the Songhai empire. He proposed to build a canal to link Timbuktu and Walata. The project was actually begun but was never finished.

The Mossi Yatenga presented a serious challenge to the growing power of Songhai under Sonni Ali. During the reign of Mansa Musa of Mali, the Mossi had made bold to raid Timbuktu and its neighbourhood. In 1480 they sacked Walata and retired after taking considerable booty. Sonni Ali pursued them about the Western Sudan until, realizing their inferiority before the Songhai army, the Mossi turned southward to their home. By then Ali had gained control over Walata.

Hombori in the wide arch formed by the northern bend of the Niger was the next scene of Sonni Ali's campaigns. After subduing Hombori he conducted a successful expedition against the Fulani rulers of Massina, north of Jenne. For ten years or so Ali had carried Songhai arms far and wide, and his fame began to spread abroad.

In 1483 Sonni Ali took up arms once more against the Mossi who were alleged to be planning an attack on Songhai. In 1485 and 1486 he followed the Mossi right to the edge of the southern forest, where he decided to go no farther. He turned his army eastward and began a campaign against Borgu. However, this time he scored only a partial victory. In 1492 Sonni Ali began the last campaign of his military career against the Fulani of Gurma between Borgu and Gao. It was a victorious expedition, but as the old soldier was returning home to his capital he was drowned while crossing a stream. Thus ended the reign of Sonni Ali, who had done for Songhai exactly what Sundiata had done for Mali two centuries earlier. Because of his harshness towards foreigners and scholars in the Western Sudan, Sonni Ali earned unkind remarks from the Arabic historians; but by all standards Ali deserved to rank as one of the greatest monarchs of Africa.

Mohammed Askia the Great
On Sonni Ali's death there followed a struggle for the succession between Ali's son, Bakari Da'a, and the late king's chief minister and supporter, Mohammed Ture. After defeating his rival at Angoo, Ture made a triumphal entry into Gao and was proclaimed king. When Sonni

Ali's daughters heard the news they are said to have cried out 'Asi kyi a' ('He shall not be!'). Ture adopted the scornful protest of the girls as his title and became known as Askia Mohammed I, thus establishing the Askia dynasty. In history Mohammed I is popularly known as Askia the Great.

Askia Mohammed I consolidated the territorial gains that Sonni Ali had made for Songhai and further extended the boundaries of the empire. The praises that the Arabic historians denied Sonni Ali they heaped upon Askia Mohammed. Mohammed was more refined in his personal tastes and habits than Ali. He showed great respect for and attention to the Islamic faith and learning in general. The learned people who had fled from Timbuktu to Walata at the time of Sonni Ali's conquest of Timbuktu now returned to the famous seat of learning. Mohammed encouraged the building of schools and mosques and a new cultural life was evident throughout the Songhai empire.

One of Askia Mohammed's greatest contributions to the political life not only of Songhai but also of the Western Sudan in general was his introduction of administrative reform. He did away with the old system of using military force to keep down the people of the countryside. He established a standing army but mainly to carry out his plans for terri- torial expansion. To facilitate the administration of an empire that was becoming more extensive he divided the whole empire into fairly clear- cut provinces, each with a governor in charge. The first was the province of *Kormina* in the west. This included parts of Mali proper, Massina, the pagan country of Bambara and the region west of the Niger stretching towards the Atlantic. The second province was *Bala*, which comprised the northern territories of the empire – Walata, Timbuktu and Taghaza in the desert. The third province was *Banku,* which covered the region lying between Timbuktu and Gao, and extended to Tekadda. Lastly, there was the province of *Dendi.* This covered a wide area incuding the Middle Niger and east of the river – Hausaland, Bornu and Agades to the north. The governor of each province was known by the old title of Koi or Fari. The native rulers of the various places were allowed to retain their positions of dignity, but were made responsible to the Koi or Fari.

Shortly after his accession Askia Mohammed I began to extend the frontiers of the empire he had inherited from his old master, Sonni Ali. However, before beginning his campaign of conquest he made a pilgrim- age to Mecca in 1495. He was attended by much fewer followers than Mansa Musa, but Askia Mohammed also displayed great wealth and spent freely in the Middle East. His small group of attendants included notable and learned men from the Western Sudan. The Sudanese pilgrims spent two years in the east, and it is said they took the opportunity of studying eastern legal and administrative methods. The Caliph of Egypt, the head of Moslems, invested Askia Mohammed as his representative in the Western Sudan. Askia Mohammed made great friends in the east. We know from various sources that he asked many questions about subjects that interested him and gathered a good deal of useful information and experience. All this no doubt guided him in his work of administrative reform and gave him the refinement of behaviour that Sonni Ali lacked.

Askia Mohammed returned to the Sudan from his pilgrimage to Mecca in 1497. Shortly afterwards he began a series of military campaigns that further extended the frontiers of the Songhai empire. His first engagement was a holy war against the Mossi to the south. This was largely successful, although Askia met with stiff resistance. He then turned west, overran Mali territory and forced the Mandingoes to pay tribute. However, the Mandingoes of Mali struck back from time to time and further campaigns by Songhai armies were needed before Mali was finally subdued. Askia also defeated the Fulani to the south-west and placed their country under Songhai control. He now turned to the north and carried Songhai arms to the salt mines of Taghaza in the desert.

After an interval of some years Askia resumed his campaign of conquest. The east and north-east were the new scenes of expansion. He began a long and successful expedition in the region stretching from the eastern frontier of Songhai on the Niger to Lake Chad. He became master of the Hausa states of Gobir, Kano, Zaria and Katsina. As a result of this successful expedition Askia acquired a rich and populous area for Songhai. The conquest of Hausaland by Askia drew him into conflict with the Tuareg living to the north. In 1515 he set out on a fresh campaign towards the north against Al Adalet, ruler of the Tuareg of Agades. He captured Agades and set up a Songhai colony. He then moved farther north to Aïr, in the desert, which also fell to him. The Songhai drove the Tuareg of Aïr into the desert, and Askia established a Songhai colony there also.

Askia had been greatly helped in his campaigns against the Hausa states and the Tuareg by Kanta, king of Kebbi. Kanta had been a most faithful ally but after the Agades campaign he became dissatisfied with his share of the spoils of war and quarrelled with Askia. Askia sent a Songhai army against Kanta, but it was defeated. Kanta, however, died in the course of the conflict and became a hero in the traditions of Kebbi.

The last years of Askia the Great were filled with suffering and humilia-
tion for the old king. His son, Musa, rebelled against him. With the
support of his brothers, Daud and Ismail, Musa set up an independent
kingdom at Kukia. Askia Mohammed, now advanced in age and blind,
was forced by his rebellious sons to abdicate in favour of Musa, in 1528.
Thus ended one of the most illustrious reigns in the history of the
Western Sudan. Askia the Great reigned for thirty-six years. The empire
he left behind extended from Bornu to the Atlantic and from the fringes of
the southern forest to Aïr in the Sahara.

After Askia the Great

Askia Musa, who had ousted his old father from the Songhai throne, was
assassinated after a short reign of three years in which he had made
himself unpopular by adopting harsh methods of rule. Musa was succeeded by Mohammed Bergan, who led an unsuccessful expedition
against Kebbi. Askia Korei succeeded Bergan on the throne. Then came
the reign of Ismail. Ismail made an unsuccessful attempt to subdue the
pagans of Ghana.

In 1543 Askia Ishak ascended the Songhai throne. His reign of six years
was one of very considerable activity. He conducted successful campaigns against the Ntoba in Dendugu in the extreme west and then
against Dendi. He reconquered the Mali, who had revolted against
Songhai domination, but although he succeeded in subduing the old
Mali capital he failed to occupy it permanently. When Ishak died in 1549,
however, he had somewhat strengthened the central government and
upheld the prestige of Songhai.

The second half of the sixteenth century was generally a period of
danger and great difficulties for Songhai. In spite of fairly successful
expeditions to suppress revolts in the empire conducted by Ishak's
successor, Askia Daud, Songhai began to show signs of weakness and
decline. Songhai was involved in a quarrel with Morocco which ended in
a Moorish invasion of the Western Sudan and the subsequent destruction of Songhai power. The conflict between Morocco and Songhai is
discussed in the next chapter.

The Mossi-Dagomba states

The country stretching from the headwaters of the Volta River to the
grassland bordering on the forest areas to the south is the home of
virile groups of people who possess a common culture and who speak
related languages. They are sometimes referred to as the Voltaic peoples.

Before considering the states to the east of the Niger it may be worthwhile to stop for a brief summary of the history of these peoples living around the Volta. In late medieval times a number of related kingdoms and states were set up among the Voltaic peoples, the most prominent being the Mossi, Dagomba and Mamprusi kingdoms. These kingdoms were neither in size nor in sophistication comparable to their imposing neighbours of Mali and Songhai to the north. However, they stood the test of time and some of them boast today of dynasties dating back five hundred years. They were never subjugated by their big northern neighbours. They not only successfully repelled Mali and Songhai attacks upon them, but they sometimes retaliated by carrying their arms right into the heart of the Mali and Songhai empires on the Niger. The Mossi, Dagomba and Mamprusi kingdoms also resolutely resisted attempts to impose the Islamic faith on them. They have for centuries remained faithful to their local gods and religious practices. The Arabic scholars who wrote about medieval Ghana, Mali and Songhai paid little or no attention to the peoples living to the south of the great Sudanese kingdoms. The peoples to the south appear vaguely in the records of the Arabic scholars as the Lem-Lems. Our knowledge of the history of the Voltaic peoples is fragmentary and largely or wholly based upon oral tradition. Some of the kingdoms have preserved complete lists of their kings, but information on the achievements of the kings is either scanty or legendary. All that is attempted here is to present a brief summary of the history of the Voltaic states as far as can be glimpsed from their traditions. As the Voltaic peoples have 'uniform religion, uniform tribal and totemic organization and an identical political constitution or system of tribal government',* a study of one or two Voltaic states should be enough to throw some light on general developments in the vast area through which the Volta runs.

One fundamental fact is the key to the understanding of the history of Mossi, Dagomba, Mamprusi and the other lesser kingdoms of the Voltaic peoples. There is in all these states a main body of old-established inhabitants who must have been living in the area for as long as history can tell. In the course of medieval times strangers arriving from outside imposed themselves upon the aboriginal peoples as a ruling aristocracy. The mass of earlier peoples were grouped into clans and ruled by priest-kings. They followed a simple pattern of life. Of these peoples Captain Rattray has written:

* Rattray, *Tribes of the Ashanti Hinterland*, Clarendon Press, Oxford, 1932, Vol. I, p. xiv.

'Wealth in our modern sense was unknown; the people went about naked; their property consisted only of bows and arrows, pots, calabashes and livestock. Disputes were settled by the Elders of each family group. The priestly ruler was appealed to only in cases affecting a breach of the tribal taboos, or in matters of wider than family import. Fear of the ancestral or other spirits moulded [their] action. . . .'*

The invaders from outside later imposed secular rule upon these peoples. The strangers, who appear to have carried out their invasion in relatively small bands, apparently of males, must have succeeded in establishing their domination over the aboriginal peoples by virtue of better military skill and superior political ability. They settled among the people they found and married their women. In the end the strangers adopted the languages of the tribes among whom they settled. In course of time the old-established inhabitants and the newcomers merged together. It is both interesting and revealing to note that in the Dagomba and Mamprusi states today there exist clan priests called the *ten'dama* who are regarded as the guardians of the land and custodians of the religious practices of their clans. The *ten'dama* are quite distinct from the territorial chiefs. A territorial chief, it is said, often describes his position thus: 'The people belong to me, the land belongs to the *'ten'-dama'*.† Apart from the new political organization which the invading bands brought, it is doubtful if they effected any remarkable changes in the daily lives of the peoples upon whom they became superimposed. For centuries after the invasion, life continued almost exactly as it was when the invaders swooped down upon the peoples. In a way, however, the strangers proved to be shrewd. Many of the tribes practised the system of tracing inheritance through the sister's son. However, the invaders realised that if they were to maintain their position as titular leaders they must 'insist on descent and inheritance through the male line as alone conferring title to the office of the territorial rulers'.‡

The remembered history of Mossi, Dagomba and Mamprusi is often the history of the ruling aristocracy. The common traditions of origin of these kingdoms centre upon a legendary leader whose name is given as Tohajie, meaning Red Hunter. He is said to have reached the Upper Region of the modern state of Ghana after several days of journey from his home in the east. Tohajie's grandson, Bawa or Gbewa, is said to have

---

* Rattray, *Tribes of the Ashanti Hinterland,* Clarendon Press, Oxford, 1932, Vol.I, p. xiv.
† In the same work, p. xv.
‡ In the same work, p. xv.

finally settled at a place called Pusiga, near Bawku. Bawa, according to popular tradition, had eight sons. When he died he was succeeded by his eldest son, Zirile. On Zirile's death a succession dispute ensued among his surviving brothers and the family was split up. One of Zirile's brothers, by name Sitobo, in the end moved out and founded the Dagomba kingdom. Another brother, Yantuare, founded the Mossi kingdom. The youngest brother, Tohogo, also became founder of the Mamprusi kingdom. Thus Mossi, Dagomba and Mamprusi claim a common origin and as a matter of fact they have been usually bound together in a sort of friendly alliance for the greater part of their subsequent history.

The invaders to whom the founding of the Mossi, Dagomba and Mamprusi kingdoms is attributed are believed to have come from the region of Lake Chad, moving westward by way of Zamfara in Hausaland. Their invasion of the Voltaic peoples is reckoned to have taken place about the fourteenth century. They are referred to in local traditions as being red and it is clear that they rode on horseback. The use of the horse must have given the invaders both military and political advantages in their state-building enterprise. The importance of the horse as the key to political power in the open savanna country of the Sudan has already been stressed earlier in this book. Today, especially in Dagomba and Mamprusi, the horse features prominently in state ceremonial and its possession accords prestige.

The land of the Voltaic peoples was frequented in early times by Mande-speaking people from Mali and Songhai. Their activities were mainly centred on trade. However, in the late sixteenth and early seventeenth centuries some Mande-speaking people mounted an invasion against the Voltaic peoples. One such invading group, led by a brilliant warrior called Jakpa, established a dynasty in Gonja to the south-west of Dagomba.

Dagomba is the most southerly of the three kingdoms and lies just outside the borders of the forest zone. The greatness of Dagomba is generally associated with the reign of Nyagse, son of Sitobo, the founder of the kingdom. Many significant military exploits are attributed to Nyagse. He made frequent wars throughout the territory that eventually came under Dagomba and he is said to have established his own kinsmen as rulers in various places after putting the original rulers to death. Nyagse's grandson marched westward against the old kingdom of Bona and conquered it, although he did not make much out of this conquest. During the reign of Dariziogo, the eleventh chief of the state, Dagomba suffered a serious check in its expansionist activities. A warrior leader of Mande origin, called Sumaila Ndwewura Jakpa, in a brilliant military career welded together the Gonja people under his rule. He captured the important salt centre of Daboya from Dagomba. He then advanced further against Dagomba and inflicted a crushing defeat on the Dagomba army under chief Dariziogo. Jakpa is supposed to have founded Salaga and other smaller towns in the area. It is estimated that Jakpa's invasion may have taken place about the year 1620. Diara had been the capital of Dagomba but after the harassment by Gonja, the Dagomba chief Luoro, who succeeded Dariziogo, set up a new capital at Yendi.

For almost a century Dagomba lived under the shadow of the menace of Gonja. During the first half of the eighteenth century, however, Azigeri succeeded in freeing Dagomba from the Gonja threat after soundly beating a Gonja army. Dagomba was able to enjoy peace for a while, but during the second half of the century the forest state of Asante in the south, taking advantage of a disputed succession in Dagomba, sent an army of invasion against the state. The Asante army was able to occupy the Dagomba capital of Yendi for a while and retired only after imposing a heavy annual tribute of slaves. Dagomba was compelled to pay the tribute for many years with the help of Mamprusi.

The various reverses suffered by the Dagomba people did not stop them from devoting themselves to external economic pursuits. The Dagomba country, like most of the neighbourhood was semi-arid and the economy in general was at subsistence level. However, Dagomba was able to constitute itself into an important link in the trade between the forest areas of the south and the Western Sudan. Acting as middlemen, the people of Dagomba carried gold and kola from the forest zone. The latter article was of particular importance. The kolanut was not only a delicacy to the Voltaic peoples and the Western Sudanese: it was also believed to have a minimizing effect on thirst and was thus considered valuable during journeys across the desert. It should be emphasized that the underlying progressive factor in the various Mossi states was the role of long-distance trade, the work of Moslems, usually Mande-Fula, who pioneered in the late medieval period trade-routes to Northern Ghana both from the north-west and to Hausaland.

There are two main branches of Mossi states – Yatenga and Wagadugu. The Mossi states were in immediate contact with both Mali and Songhai, but they were never incorporated in the Sudanese empires. It is not very clear when the invaders from the east began to organize Yatenga and Wagadugu into political states, but by the early fourteenth century the Yatenga at least were already a strong force with which Mali had to contend. In c.1333, barely a year after the death of Mansa Musa of Mali, the Mossi Yatenga marched upon Timbuktu and sacked the town after surprising and routing the Mandingo garrison stationed there. The Mossi appear to have carried out this act of hostility almost with impunity, for no serious reprisal came from Mali. After this bold act the Mossi were not heard of again in the bend of the Niger till the reign of Sonni Ali of Songhai in the fifteenth century. The series of successful military campaigns waged by Sonni Ali must have made the Mossi restless and excited. In 1480 the Yatenga were again on the warpath in the bend of the Niger. They marched north-west this time and succeeded in capturing Walata on the edge of the desert after a siege which is said to have lasted for a month. They sacked the town and carried off women and children as well as considerable booty. This was very disturbing news to Sonni Ali, who was at the time engaged in a process of mastering the whole region west and north-west of Timbuktu. However, Sonni Ali was not the man to overlook the Mossi threat and in fact he lost no time in dislodging the Yatenga from what he claimed to be his territory. The Mossi, fleeing from Sonni Ali, fell foul of Mali, which no longer constituted a serious military force. It is said that the Mali implored the help of the Portuguese against the Mossi but without success. The Portuguese were by this time active on the Guinea Coast and had established a trade post at Wadan in the hinterland of Cape Blanco.

During the reign of Askia the Great the Yatenga were again showing signs of hostility to Songhai, and Askia had to make war on them. He had just returned from a pilgrimage to Mecca and was able to cloak his invasion of the Mossi with the pretext of a holy war aimed at their paganism. The Moorish invasion of the Songhai empire and the consequent destruction of Songhai power followed by the disintegration of the empire rid the Mossi of a strong punitive hand. An interesting fact about the history of the Mossi is that they were able to remain masters of their own lands until the advent of French colonial rule towards the end of the nineteenth century.

5 The Moroccan invasion of the Western Sudan

Relations between Morocco and Songhai

The Moroccan invasion of the Western Sudan which began in 1590 was the work of the young sultan or ruler of Morocco, Mulay Ahmed, also known as El Mansur, who ascended the Moroccan throne in 1578. In invading the Western Sudan it was the aim of Mulay Ahmed to gain control over the source of the trans-Saharan gold trade; but prevailing circumstances in Morocco urged him greatly in his decision. A few months before Mulay Ahmed became ruler of Morocco his country had been invaded by Portugal. The Portuguese expedition to Morocco which resulted from the ambition of Sebastian, the king of Portugal, was very badly managed. Sebastian's army was a motley crowd numbering some 25,000 men largely made up of mercenaries who had been released from religious wars that had been raging in Germany for years. His cavalry was contemptible. The Portuguese army suffered a humiliating defeat by the Moroccans at the decisive battle of El Kasr el Kibir. It is said that only a few hundred Portuguese escaped slaughter. The reigning sultan or ruler of Morocco died in the moment of the Moroccan victory over the Portuguese and was succeeded by his younger brother, Mulay Ahmed. Ahmed, who had played a brilliant part in the Moroccan victory, was given an additional name, El Mansur, meaning The Victorious.

Like many men after gaining great victories, Mulay Ahmed El Mansur was filled with great confidence. The decisive battle at El Kasr el Kibir had in fact brought to an end the dream of European conquest in North Africa. The twenty-nine-year-old sultan had gained a position of immense prestige. Ambassadors from England, France, Spain and Turkey came to his court. He was determined to encourage commerce and industry in Morocco. He had at his disposal a large army and soon began to look for further fields of conquest. A Moroccan invasion of the Iberian peninsula would have been a rash proposition, for even in her apparent decadent state at the time, Spain was still a formidable military power. Expansion over the North African coast was also out of the question, for the Turks were in control of it, and moreover Morocco itself was under threat by them. It was in expansion southward to the Western Sudan alone that El Mansur saw his chance. This possibility was economically attractive: for many years Morocco, at the northern end of an important trans-Saharan trade-route, had wanted to gain as much as possible of the gold from the Western Sudan, particularly in the course of the sixteenth century.

Possession of the salt mines of Taghaza would have given Morocco a most valuable commodity in exchange for Sudanese gold. Taghaza had passed under the control of Songhai during the reign of Askia the Great. Evidently this did not please the rulers of Morocco. The first signs of friction between Morocco and Songhai over Taghaza showed themselves during the reign of Askia Ishak. In 1546 Mulay el Aarejd, the sultan or ruler of Morocco, had asked Ishak to cede Taghaza to Morocco. Ishak not only refused to hand over Taghaza but warned the sultan not to repeat the request by sending a force of 2,000 Tuareg under his control to raid the country of Dra'a just south of Morocco. In reply to this warlike act on the part of Songhai the Sultan of Morocco sent a body of Moroccans to attack Taghaza. The Moroccans killed the Songhai governor of Taghaza and a number of Tuareg engaged in the salt trade with the Western Sudan. In 1957 the Songhai and Tuareg salt dealers of Taghaza were forced to open a new salt mine at a place called Taghaza al Gislem, half-way between Taghaza and Taodeni.

In 1578 Mulay Ahmed El Mansur succeeded to the throne of Morocco. Like his predecessor, El Mansur requested the king of Songhai, Askia Daud, to lease to him the salt mines of Taghaza for a year. He made Daud a handsome present of 10,000 gold pieces. When Askia Daud died in 1582 he was succeeded by his son Muhammed El Hadj. El Mansur sent Moroccan envoys to present gifts to El Hadj and to congratulate him on becoming king of Songhai. The new Songhai king received the Moroccan envoys with kindness and enthusiasm and made a return gift to El Mansur. The concealed purpose of the presence of the Moroccans in the Western Sudan was really to spy in preparation for a contemplated Moroccan invasion of Songhai.

After the return of his envoys to the Western Sudan, El Mansur sent a large Moroccan force arcoss the desert to attack Wadan situated southeast of Mauritania. In 1585 another Moroccan force of about 200 men armed with muskets seized Taghaza as well as the new salt mines at Taghaza el Gizlem. Songhai forces succeeded in regaining Taghaza, but Songhai control of the mines does not appear to have been fully reestablished. The salt mines of Taodeni now became the chief source of salt supply to the Songhai empire. El Mansur appears to have lost his nerve a little, for he announced his willingness to abandon his designs on Taghaza if Askia Ishak II, the new king of Songhai, would pay him a levy in gold on every load of salt that was carried from the mines into the Sudan. Ishak II refused.

The clash in the Upper Niger
A treacherous act by a Songhai man gave El Mansur a pretext to carry out his plan to invade Songhai. In 1589 a Songhai called Uld Kirimfil arrived at El Mansur's capital, Marrakech. Uld had been banished by the king of Songhai to Taghaza for misconduct. Presenting himself before El Mansur, Uld declared that he was a Songhai prince and heir to the Songhai throne, whose position Askia Ishak II had usurped. He appealed to El Mansur to restore him to the Songhai throne. El Mansur was not slow in seizing the opportunity, but when he placed before his council of state his plan to invade Songhai, the councillors unanimously expressed their disapproval, pointing out the difficulties of an invading army marching across the desert and the dangers involved in an unsuccessful invasion. El Mansur brushed their fears aside and decided to go ahead with his plan.

For the invasion of the Western Sudan El Mansur collected an army of 4,000 soldiers made up largely of European mercenaries. The men were carefully selected for their bravery and their ability to bear the hardship of a long march across the Sahara. The army consisted of 2,000 infantry, 500 horsemen and 1,500 lancers. Some 8,000 camels and 1,000 pack-horses were to transport the army, its equipment and provisions to the Sudan. The army of invasion of the Western Sudan is said to have been the most efficient that Morocco ever assembled. El Mansur selected a faithful servant, a Spanish Arab and an eunuch called Judar to command the army. We shall henceforth refer to Judar by his full title Judar Pasha.

On the 16th October 1590 the Moroccan force under Judar Pasha set out for the Western Sudan, a journey of nearly 1,500 miles. It took the Sijilmasa-Taghaza-Walata caravan route. There is no clear record of the experience of the Moroccan expedition across the desert. Various accounts of its numbers that perished while crossing the desert have come down to us, but none appears very reliable. Probably many of the Moroccans died of thirst or of exhaustion. By the end of 1590 the Moroccans under Judar Pasha had reached the Niger at Karabara.

When Ishak II and the Songhai heard of the approach of the Moroccan army, it seems they did not take prompt action to deal with it. Probably they thought the Sahara would take care of the expedition. A council held by Askia Ishak II to consider what was to be done ended in confusion. At last Ishak decided to send messengers to the desert to fill in the wells so that the Moroccans might perish on the way. However, the messengers fell into the hands of some desert robbers so that they could not carry out their mission.

The first clash between the Moroccans and the Songhai took place at a place called Tondibi. Askia Ishak II put into the field a large Songhai force, but it must be borne in mind that the Songhai soldiers armed mainly with bows and arrows were at a very serious disadvantage fighting against the Moroccans carrying muskets and a few pieces of heavy artillery. The odds were against the Songhai: their army was for the most part a rabble. When the battle opened, Askia Ishak II tried a simple strategy. He ordered his men to let loose a large herd of cattle into the Moroccan army. The Moroccans, however, opened their ranks and the cattle rushed by, doing no harm. Then the Songhai were slaughtered. Askia, quickly despairing, sent orders to the people of Gao to cross the Niger and seek safety in Gurma. Many of them were drowned in the general panic to cross the river and in the absence of sufficient boats. The battle of Tondibi should go down as one of the most remarkable conflicts in the history of the Western Sudan. Askia and his army also fled across the Niger after sending orders to Timbuktu for the people to do the same. The Songhai had lost the first engagement with the Moroccans – the Battle of Tondibi.

Judar Pasha and his army entered Gao unopposed, but the Moroccans were greatly disappointed. Most of the inhabitants of Gao had fled, leaving hardly any valuable property behind for the Moroccans to loot. The foreign merchants of Gao who had refused to flee, together with a few native inhabitants, were on hand to welcome the Moroccan army. It must be noted that as far as is known this engagement marks the first use of firearms in the Western Sudan. From popular accounts that they had heard in North Africa, the Moroccans had fancied Gao to be a prosperous city of great architectural beauty. They found only mud huts roofed with thatch. Even Askia's own house was as simple as the ordinary houses of the town. Above all there was no gold to be had. It was little realized in Morocco and in North Africa in general, that although the gold mines in the Western Sudan were accessible to Ghana, Mali and Songhai successively, they were located farther south.

After the Moroccans had occupied Gao, Ishak II opened negotiations with Judar Pasha. He offered to give the Moroccans about 12,500 ounces of gold and a thousand slaves if they would leave the Western Sudan and go home to Morocco. He further conceded to Morocco the right to import salt and cowries into the Western Sudan, thus virtually handing over control of the trans-Saharan trade to the Moroccans. However, Judar Pasha had no authority to accept such terms, even if obviously favourable, without reference to the Sultan back in Morocco. He therefore despatched a messenger to Morocco to place the terms before El Mansur and to learn his desire. Ishak II, anxious to get rid of the Moroccans from Gao, suggested to Judar Pasha that he might move his soldiers to more healthy Timbuktu, offering to provide the Moroccans with horses for transport. Judar subsequently retired to Timbuktu. The inhabitants of Timbuktu received their Moroccan guests very coldly. Judar pulled down the buildings in a quarter of Timbuktu to make a camp for his soldiers.

Judar's messenger carrying the terms of the peace negotiations to El Mansur reached Marrakech in June 1591. El Mansur would not hear of the terms. He was furious that Judar had allowed himself to be tricked out of Gao by Ishak. The enraged Sultan appointed a new commander in the person of a trusted servant, Mahmud ben Zergun (Mahmud Pasha), to supersede Judar in the Sudan. Mahmud left for the Sudan at once with reinforcements. He reached the Sudan seven weeks after setting out from Marrakech and immediately took over the command of the Moroccan force from Judar.

Ishak had meanwhile reorganized his forces and was able to encounter Mahmud Pasha at Bamba. But Askia was again forced to flee across the Niger, taking his army into Gurma. In the general confusion of defeat and retreat, Ishak II became separated from the main body of his soldiers and the luckless Askia was murdered by wandering tribesmen believed to be Tuareg.

Askia Nuh

Mohammed Gao, a trusted minister of Askia Ishak II, was elected to succeed his luckless master. Gao decided that the best thing to do was to submit to the Sultan of Morocco. Invited by the Moroccans to their camp, Askia Gao was treacherously arrested and taken to Judar in Gao, where he was murdered. After Gao's death the Moroccans appointed their own Askia and installed him in Timbuktu, which they declared the new capital of Songhai. However, the Songhai insisted on their independence and chose their own king. Henceforth there were two Askias – one in the north, a puppet of the Moroccans, and the other, the true choice of independent Songhai, in the south.

A brilliant national leader arose to lead the Songhai in their most trying situation in the person of Nuh, a younger brother of Mohammed Gao. After he had been proclaimed Askia, Nuh engaged the Moroccans in hit-and-run warfare for the next four years. He avoided open battles and resorted to guerilla activities. But at last he was compelled to withdraw southward to the edge of the forest. Mahmud Pasha followed Nuh south until the thick bush forced the Moroccans to give up the chase. Nuh soon returned to the struggle and the Songhai and the Moroccans came face to face in Borgu. Nuh again avoided an open battle and returned to his guerilla tactics. Disease broke out among the Moroccans and hampered their activities. For two years Mahmud fruitlessly followed the Songhai. He knew he would never win a decisive victory and decided to despatch a report to El Mansur explaining the general difficulties which faced the Moroccans in the Sudan. El Mansur received the report with sympathy but resolved that the Songhai forces must be crushed at all costs. He ordered a fresh force of 1,500 Moroccan soldiers to march into the Sudan.

Meanwhile Mahmud Pasha carried on his campaign against Nuh. Nuh and his soldiers fled from the Niger valley into the mountains of Hombori. Mahmud Pasha was killed in an attempt to get at Nuh in the mountainous district where he had entrenched himself. Nuh soon afterwards met his death also at the hands of a Moroccan force that had pressed on with the attack after Mahmud had been killed. With the passing away of the two opposing leaders, Mahmud Pasha and Askia Nuh, the heroic part of the conflict came to an end.

The rest of the story of the Moroccan invasion of the Western Sudan is a sad one for both the Songhai and the Moroccans. The sultan of Morocco still continued to send reinforcements and new commanders into the Sudan, but although the power of the Songhai had been broken, the Moroccans could not gain a hold over the southern regions of the Songhai empire. For several decades in the seventeenth century the Moroccans remained in the north, especially the Timbuktu area. The Moroccans in the Sudan began to show little regard for the central authority in Morocco. They quarrelled and fought among themselves, became brutal in their dealings with the local populations and failed to provide an orderly government in that part of the Sudan where they claimed to be masters.

Results of the Moroccan invasion

Es-Sadi, the native Sudanese historian, writing in the seventeenth century, summed up the effects of the Moroccan invasion of the Western Sudan in these sad words:

'Security gave place to danger, wealth to poverty, distress and calamities, and violence succeeded tranquility. Everywhere men destroyed each other; in every place and in every direction there was plundering, and war spared neither property nor persons. Disorder was general and spread everywhere, rising to the highest degree of intensity'. These words are in complete contrast to Ibn Batuta's account concerning the general peace and security in the Western Sudan during the fourteenth century in the days of Mali.

The great prosperity and tranquility evident in the Middle Niger in particular and in the Western Sudan in general before the Moroccan invasion was the product of a strong central government provided by Songhai. The Moroccan invasion destroyed this stability, and a general confusion followed. To the Songhai empire the immediate sequel of the Moroccan invasion was disintegration. The strong hand of Songhai alone had kept together a great diversity of Sudanese peoples. The defeat of the Songhai army at Tondibi was followed by a general outbreak of violence and lawlessness. The news of Askia Ishak II's flight was a signal for the various tribes and peoples under the control of Songhai to revolt and proclaim their independence. For example, the Fulani began to raid and ravage the countryside around Timbuktu. The pagan Bambara fell upon the rich province of Jenne. The Tuareg, who had been kept in check by the fear of Songhai authority, broke loose on the Sudanese peasantry north of the Niger. It seems that with the destruction of the authority of Songhai all the worst elements in the Western Sudan began to show themselves.

The last decade of the sixteenth century did not only witness the spread of war and destruction in the Western Sudan. The exorbitant taxes imposed by the Moroccans helped to destroy the prosperity of the Sudan. The trans-Saharan trade declined in the seventeenth century. The Moorish leaders in the Sudan placed heavy levies on the merchants in an attempt to find the money to pay for the cost of their campaigns and to justify the invasion of the Western Sudan in the eyes of the public of Morocco. After failing to find gold in the quantities he had hoped for,

El Mansur in a fury ordered the arrest and transportation of many scholars in Timbuktu together with their books to Morocco where they remained prisoners for a good many years. The cultural life of the Sudan thus suffered. Es-Sadi again bemoans the situation thus:

'The worst of the common people were preferred to the most noble; the rule of justice was supressed; tradition became a dead letter; no one observed the law nor walked in the fear of God.'

On the whole the Moorish invasion of the Western Sudan may be considered as a disappointing affair to Morocco. The material culture of the Sudan in general was below what El Mansur had been led to believe. The Moroccans never had access to the goldfields in the Sudan. At first, however, a good deal of gold seems to have poured into Morocco. El Mansur was able to pay his troops with coins of pure gold. It is interesting to note also that El Mansur acquired the title of El Dhahabi, meaning The Golden. It seems that his Sudanese conquests increased his wealth considerably. In 1594 an English resident in Morocco observed that thirty mules laden with gold from the Sudan arrived in Marrakech. However, there is little doubt that the disastrous effect of the Moorish invasion on the trans-Saharan trade more or less counterbalanced the wealth in the form of gold that Morocco received from the Sudan. The normal trans-Saharan trade of the seventeenth century was less than that of the previous century.

It also seems doubtful if good use was made, on the whole, of the wealth that the Sultan of Morocco gained from the Sudan beyond what was devoted to military works at Fez. The condition of the ordinary people of Morocco was no better than it had been before the invasion of the Sudan. All the Sudanese wealth that reached Morocco passed into the hands of the Sultan and a few nobles, who spent it on luxuries. El Mansur was an extravagant man who used the Sudanese wealth mainly in building luxurious castles. On the whole the fruits of the Moorish campaigns in the Western Sudan proved a doubtful boon in Morocco.

The Moors in the Western Sudan after 1600

The Moors did by no means master the Songhai empire; they only tried to rule the middle of the Niger bend, the region around Timbuktu and Gao. After the death of Askia Nuh in about 1599, the Songhai of Dendi never again made any serious attempt to recover what they had lost to the Moroccans. However, the struggle against Nuh had made it clear to the Moroccans that they could not conquer Dendi. Nevertheless, fighting still continued on a minor scale for ten years or more. In 1608 the Hi Koi of Dendi attacked the Moroccans on the Upper Niger. In the following year the Moroccans were called upon to repel an attack on Jenne by the Songhai. In 1612 a Songhai army appeared before Timbuktu but was defeated. Far into the seventeenth century the Moroccans were attacked by the Songhai at various points.

Meanwhile among the Moors in the Sudan there was developing great confusion. After the death of El Mansur In 1603 the Moors in the Sudan were no longer inclined to take orders from Morocco. The Moroccan troops made and unmade pashas in the Sudan. Between 1612 and 1621 there were no less than twenty-one pashas. As time went on the Moroccans lost their military qualities. They married Sudanese women and from the union emerged a class of mulattoes called the Armar.

Why did the Moors fail to hold the Western Sudan? Although they could not conquer the southern regions of the Songhai empire, their victory in the north was clear. However, they failed to maintain the north as a dominion of Morocco. The remoteness of the Sudan was largely responsible for this failure. The Sudan was separated from Morocco by more than 1,500 miles of desert. Communication between the two was a real problem. Two to three months would elapse before a reply to a despatch from the Sudan was received from Marrakech. A practical way out of the difficulty of communication would have been a considerable degree of discretion for the pashas in the Sudan as the men on the spot. Such a development the sultan would not allow. The pashas were required to refer all matters of importance and even relatively unimportant ones to Marrakech for final decision. This naturally weakened Moroccan administration in the Sudan. By the time the wishes of the sultan were known in the Sudan the original situation might have so altered that a fresh mandate was necessary. Orders would be out of date by the time they reached the Sudan.

The remoteness of the Western Sudan and the over-centralization of authority in Morocco greatly hampered Moroccan administration in the Sudan. An equally important cause of failure was the conduct of the Moors in the Sudan. The pashas and their lieutenants were corrupt. The troops broke into hostile and ungovernable factions. Many of the troops, though fine soldiers, were dishonest men and fortune hunters. They placed their own interests before anything else. Struggle for power and intrigue destroyed all possibilities of stable government. What the Moroccan administration in the Sudan suffered was the common fate of far-flung dominions left largely in the hands of adventurous soldiers.

C

6 Bornu

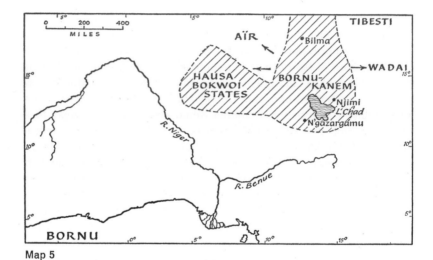

Map 5

Early history

The medieval kingdom of Bornu or Kanem-Bornu, as it is sometimes called, brings us to the eastern limits of the Western Sudan. The compound name Kanem-Bornu points to the development of the kingdom that flourished around Lake Chad. Kanem to the east of the lake remained for several centuries the heart of the kingdom; but from about the middle of the fifteenth century Bornu to the west of the lake replaced Kanem as the centre of power. We may for the sake of convenience call the earlier period dominated by Kanem as the first Kanuri or Bornu empire and the later period dominated by Bornu as the second empire. Some historians avoid the compound term Kanem-Bornu and simply use Bornu for the kingdom of two centres of influence. This example is followed here.

The kingdom of Bornu started about the eighth century A.D., that is, about the time when Ghana was entering upon its heyday, and lasted for a thousand years. It should be noted that the present Bornu Province of Northern Nigeria represents only a small part of the medieval kingdom of Bornu. The massive territory under Bornu, when the kingdom was at its peak, was in shape roughly like an avocado pear with its bottom sitting on Lake Chad, pointing northward into the desert and holding within its apex the great caravan centre of Bilma (see Map 5).

The most important people living around Lake Chad, the heart of the kingdom of Bornu, are the Kanuri or the Kanembu, as they are sometimes called. To the east of Lake Fitri live the Bulala, a tribe akin to the Kanuri. But the aboriginal people of old Bornu and Kanem were a collection of Negro tribes known as the So. The So at first lived on the eastern side of Lake Chad, but in the twelfth and thirteenth centuries they moved to the country west of the lake.

The history of Bornu has been greatly influenced by the shallow waters of Lake Chad. This enormous sheet of water, in spite of its swampy banks, has been a special attraction to the nomadic dwellers of the southern Sahara. The geographical position of Bornu is thus the key to its history. From early times nomadic tribes from the desert had converged on the Lake Chad basin. At first they were content to drive their beasts to the fertile region for short periods, finally retiring to their desert abodes. However, the attractions offered by the congenial conditions of the Chad basin offered an irresistible invitation to them for permanent occupation. The desert nomads possessed the advantage of political and possibly military skill over the aboriginal tribes.

The lake region had a number of links with the outside world. From early times an important caravan route linked it and Tripoli in North Africa through Murzuk in the Fezzan and through Bilma in the southern Sahara. It was linked also by an indirect route with Cairo. The Chad basin besides provided an important meeting place between the two halves of the Sudan. Whatever influences from the Nile valley reached the Western Sudan as a whole first made their appearance around Lake Chad. It was a focal point where men of different races and cultures met and mixed.

The Zaghawa, whose influence in the Western Sudan has already been noted in Chapter One, appeared in Bornu during the eighth or ninth century A.D. After establishing themselves as a ruling aristocracy they gradually mixed blood with the pre-existing Negro peoples of the area. The eventual outcome of the mixture of races was an amalgamation of cultures and the creation of a mixed population that came to be known as the Kanuri.

The first Kanuri empire

The most outstanding of the nomadic groups who entered the Chad region in early medieval times were the Beni-Sef. Under a leader called Dugu (c. A.D. 774) they set up a state and then began the Sef dynasty of Bornu that lasted for about a thousand years. The first Sef capital was N'jimi in Kanem east of the lake. The Sef kings were known by the title Mai.

Islam reached Bornu during the eleventh century, but it is not known for certain the circumstances in which the faith was introduced. It is known, however, that the first Moslem king of Bornu was Hume (1085–1097),* the tenth ruler of the Sef dynasty. It is thought that Islam was introduced into Bornu by men from Egypt. It is, however, probable that Islam reached Bornu from the Western Sudan. The successors of Hume enthusiastically embraced the Islamic faith and the pilgrimage to Mecca became an important feature of Bornu royalty. Koranic law and the Moslem system of administration spread in the kingdom. Islamic learning and culture became firmly established in Bornu.

In the middle of the eleventh century El Bekri had described the Lake Chad region as a country of pagans and difficult of access. When Idrisi, another well-known Arabic scholar, wrote about Bornu after the introduction of Islam, he said so much about the kingdom that it becomes clear that, within a century after its acceptance of Islam, Bornu had come into the orbit of the Arabic world. After making the pilgrimage to Mecca, Hume and his successors surrounded themselves with Islamic scholars. In Bornu the introduction of Islam led in broad outline to the developments already discussed in connexion with Mali and Songhai. It was in the course of the thirteenth century that Islam became firmly established in Bornu, notably among the ruling classes. However, it was always Islam of the Sudanese type: there was considerable modification of practice to suit local moods. In Bornu, for example, a person who committed murder

---

* Different dates appear in different sources for the Bornu rulers. All dates appearing in this section should be treated as approximate and taken as broad guides to the reigns.

was handed over to the family of the victim contrary to normal Islamic practice. Having accepted Islam, Bornu became a centre for its transmission and its attendant cultural developments to areas far and near. Bornu, which controlled the trade route eastward to Darfur, was probably responsible for the introduction of Islam into the country during the fifteenth century.

Hume was succeeded as king of Bornu by Dunama (c.1097–1150). Dunama is said to have made the pilgrimage three times to Mecca, on each occasion accompanied by a large body of followers. It appears that he was in the end drowned by the Egyptians at Suez because, it is suspected, they were jealous of his growing power and influence in the Middle East. During the succeeding reigns of Biri (c.1151–1176) and Selma (c.1194–1220) friendly relations were established and maintained between Bornu and Tunisia on the North African coast. During the reign of Dunama III (c.1221–1259), who is described as a warlike and restless prince, a Bornu embassy continued to be maintained in Tunisia. Bornu interests in Cairo and in pilgrimage to Mecca were alive during this period, for we are told that a hostel was built in Cairo for the use of Bornu pilgrims and students resident in the Egyptian capital. There was contact between Bornu and the peoples in the savanna-land to the west. There is mention of the arrival of Fulani teachers in Bornu towards the end of the thirteenth century.

From the middle of the thirteenth century to the end of the fourteenth there raged a bitter struggle between the Kanuri and the So, the group of aboriginal tribes to whom reference has been made earlier. The So displayed great courage and ferocity, for it is said that they were able to kill four Kanuri kings in succession. About the same time the Bulala also began to harass the Kanuri. The Bulala, akin to the Kanuri, had established themselves east of Lake Fitri whence they began to spread their influence and power.

During the reign of Mai Daud (c.1366–1376) the affairs of Bornu became complicated by the outbreak of civil war in the royal family. In the end Daud was driven out of N'jimi, his capital, and was finally killed by the Bulala. Mai Umar ibn Idris (c.1384–88), finding himself utterly unable to defend his kingdom against the Bulala, decided to move the seat of his government from the east (that is, Kanem) to the west (Bornu proper) of Lake Chad. Idris virtually fled from N'jimi. Many members of the royal family followed the example of the Mai and fled to the west. In the west the Sef dynasty was able eventually to re-establish itself firmly in the rich province of Bornu proper at N'gazargamu under Mai Ali Ghaji (c.1472–1504). At N'gazargamu the second Kanuri empire began.

Internal organization

Before entering upon what may be regarded as the modern period of the history of Bornu we may turn to the broad outlines of the internal organization of the Bornu kingdom. The kingdom was run like a large estate under the control of the ruling class on feudal lines. The feudal lords of Bornu developed considerable power and influence around their own personages. The Mai or king ruled through a Council of Twelve who determined to a large extent what the royal policy should be. The queen mother, known by the title of Magira, was responsible for the domestic arrangements of the court. She exercised control over the Mai. The Magira, it is said, could even veto a decision of the Mai's. One Magira, according to an old Bornu record, put a Mai into prison for being lax with the enforcement of Moslem law. Another influential personality in the kingdom of Bornu was the Mai's senior wife, who was known by the title Gumsu. In spite of the various checks and balances to the exercise of his authority, the Mai was treated with great reverence by his subjects.

The Kanuri or Bornu empire was divided into provinces. Each province had a governor appointed from the royal court from among the royal family. Two of the provincial governors wielded enormous powers and stood in special relationship with the Mai. The first was the Yerima, who controlled the Yeri or the northern districts against attacks by the Tuareg of the desert; the second was the Galadima, who had oversight of the districts to the south.

The Mai's territories and dominions may be divided into two groups. First, there was what may be termed national territory; and secondly the tributary or conquered territory; the latter lay beyond the borders of the former. The tributary lands were bound to the kingdom by loose ties. They paid tribute but enjoyed considerable local independence. They were, however, generally subjected to slave raids conducted by the nobles of the Mai's court from time to time. The main function of royal officials in tributary lands was to collect tribute and taxes on behalf of the Mai. There was, by and large, little sign of effective governance from the Mai's court in the outer provinces of the empire. The contact between the royal court and the tributary lands was hardly more than organized extortion. On the whole the day to day government in the outer provinces was little interfered with by the Mai's officers. The administration of justice was left in the hands of malams who lived with the local chiefs as principal advisers.

The second Kanuri empire

The new capital of N'gazargamu lay on the present border between the Federal Republic of Nigeria and the Niger Republic. N'gazargamu remained the capital of Bornu until its capture and destruction by the Fulani in 1812. Ali Ghaji put an end to the civil wars which had so weakened his kingdom and began to reform its administration. He put new enthusiasm into the practice of the Moslem faith by his own devoted example. He raised a large army for internal security. Having put his own house in order, Ali Ghaji began to wage wars on neighbouring territories. He applied his energies so much to fighting that he acquired the title El Ghazi, meaning The Warrior. He finally subjugated the Bulala. Ali Ghaji invaded Hausaland and put a number of the Hausa States, including Kano, to tribute; and he marched far north into the desert and established Bornu control over Tibesti.

Ali was anxious to develop commerce in his kingdom. During his reign Bornu became important in the trans-Saharan trade. Bornu exchanged slaves for horses from North Africa. During the fifteenth century Bornu was really beginning to achieve international recognition, for it found a place on world maps prepared by the Portuguese towards the end of the century.

Ali was succeeded by a worthy ruler in the person of Idris Kata-Karmabi (c.1504–26). Idris completed the subjugation of the Bulala. His successful campaigns against them brought him back to the old capital of N'jimi. A few years later he launched an attack on Kebbi but had to retreat. However, Idris found time for peaceful pursuits. He took trouble to cultivate diplomatic relations with North Africa, for we are told that in 1512 he sent an embassy to Tripoli.

During the reign of Mohammed (c.1524–45), who followed Idris, the Bulala rose again against Kanuri rule but were ruthlessly suppressed and their king was put to death. When Mohammed settled down to rule after the suppression of the Bulala revolt, it seems he did not have much fancy for life at N'gazargamu and attempted to establish a new capital at a place called Lade, but he did not succeed. Mohammad's reign was of considerable importance to Bornu. An old Bornu record states that 'the kingdom [of Bornu] reached under Mohammed the highest pitch of its greatness'.

Idris Aloma (1580–1617?)

The greatest name in the history of Bornu during the second Kanuri

empire is that of Idris Aloma. Before he finally assumed full responsibility for the government, the queen-mother, Magira Aicha, had maintained control of the affairs of the kingdom. It is believed that Aloma was
greatly inspired by the counsel of the queen-mother. One of Aloma's
first acts on becoming king was to send an embassy to Tripoli, it is said,
on the advice of the queen-mother. As a result of this gesture Idris
Aloma obtained a small force of Turkish musketeers with firearms to
boost his own army. He also established a force of cavalry. With his
newly equipped army Aloma was able to undertake numerous aggressive
campaigns. He attacked the So strongholds which had stood in the way
of the complete unification of Bornu. He was in the end able to besiege
and capture the So stronghold of Damasak. He then led an army against
the Tetala described as 'a warlike and high-spirited people settled in the
neighbourhood and on the islands of Lake Chad'. The spear-bearing
Tetala were no match for Aloma's soldiers armed with muskets, and they
had finally to withdraw into the swamps of the lake.

Aloma then turned westward against Kano but could only win a partial
victory on account of the strong resistance offered by the Hausa with the
stockades around Kano. Moving on from Kano, Aloma proceeded north-
west against the Tuareg of the desert right up to Aïr. His greatest victory
in the north was the occupation of the important trans-Saharan trade
centre of Bilma by the Bornuese army. After returning home, Aloma
struck to the south and the east on further successful campaigns. His
efficient army always gave him victory.

Like his great predecessors, Idris Aloma was able to devote himself
to peaceful pursuits. Probably in the ninth year of his reign he undertook
the pilgrimage to Mecca, where he built a hostel for the comfort of Bornu
pilgrims. At home he tried to enforce Moslem law at the expense of local
customary practice. The qadi (Moslem magistrates) in Aloma's time
were entrusted with the trial of all important cases. Aloma improved
N'gazargamu by the construction of brick buildings to replace the old
reed ones. No doubt the second Bornu empire reached its peak under
Idris Aloma who, according to the Bornu chronicle, 'promoted the
prosperity of the country and the wealth of the town'. The great German
scholar and traveller Barth paid tribute to Idris Aloma in the following words: 'Altogether Idris Aloma appears to have been an excellent
prince, uniting in himself the most opposite qualities: warlike energy
combined with mildness and intelligence; courage with circumspection
and patience; severity with pious feeling'.

Bornu after Aloma

Unfortunately Idris Aloma was succeeded by less able kings. His son and heir Mohammad (c. 1603–18) was not very enterprising. Ali Ibn Alhaj Umar (c. 1645–84), described as a valiant and intelligent man, provided some vigour in the running of affairs of the Bornu empire. Under Umar, N'gazargamu became a great centre of culture and learning. He renewed attacks on the Tuareg of the desert, but he appears to have been the only outstanding king of the time.

At the end of the eighteenth century Bornu still held hegemony over a wide area embracing various groups of people. It controlled vast areas east, west and south of Lake Chad. Its influence to the north reached as far as the Fezzan. But unfortunately there is a dearth of details of events in the empire during the eighteenth century. It appears that the empire was passing though a period of decline. It has been suggested that the Bornu empire, like other parts of the Western Sudan, was suffering from the aftermath of the Moroccan invasion and conquest of Songhai. Whatever the cause, things were not going well for Bornu in the eighteenth century. The empire came under strong pressure of attacks from outside as well as from internal revolts. For example the Tuareg harassed the empire, and within the empire itself some of the subject territories fought successfully for their independence. Even the once fine Bornu army lost its fighting power and could not hold the position of Bornu against the many destructive forces at work. The Mai Ahmad (1793–1810) led a military expedition against the people of Mandana in the south, but we are told that his army perished. There was, however, one comfort for Bornu in its military and political decline: as a centre of Islamic culture Bornu still retained its reputation in the Sudan.

7 The Hausa States

It has been pointed out in Chapter Two that strictly speaking there is no Hausa race: there are Hausa-speaking peoples. However, the name Hausa is loosely used for the mixed tribes that speak the Hausa language. Even in 1520 when Leo Africanus wrote about the states of the Western Sudan, by which time Islam had penetrated Hausaland, the word Hausa was not employed. Rather he referred to 'Gober' as the language of Zaria or Katsina. Thus the origin of the Hausa people cannot be traced through the name by which they are known today. The Hausa live in the vast region lying between Bauchi and the southern fringes of the Sahara and stretching from the Niger eastward toward Lake Chad. In this wide and fertile region were established in the late Middle Ages a number of related states commonly known as the Hausa States. There were two sets of Hausa States, each made up of seven states. The first is known by the term Hausa Bokwoi, that is to say, the seven true or original Hausa States. The other seven states, not truly or originally Hausa, but somehow related to the Hausa Bokwoi, are called the Banza Bokwoi, meaning the 'bastard' Hausa States (Map 6, p. 78).

The origin of the Hausa, like that of many Sudanese peoples, is difficult to locate, and so we have to rely upon a mass of oral traditions and post-jihad records – the *Zaria* and *Kano Chronicles* – for any evidence that might locate the origin of the Hausa. One such tradition – the Daura Tradition – has many variants. According to one variant, Daura was the heart or spiritual centre of the Hausa kingdom said to have been founded by Abu Yazid, son of the king of Bagdad. With a large number of followers he is said to have reached Bornu where the leading persons among his followers became disloyal. He escaped to Daura by night, and while there killed a serpent in a well outside the town. The prowess earned him a privileged position in the community, and eventually he married Daurana, the queen of Daura. Their first son was named Bawu who bore seven sons whose names were given to the seven Hausa States collectively known as the Hausa Bokwoi.

Another variant makes Abayejidu the father of the seven Hausa kingdoms. He was the son of Abdulahi, king of Bagadaza or Bagdad, driven to Bornu by a woman called Ziduvan. Abayejidu's stay in Bornu was anything but peaceful because of his warring tendencies towards the neighbouring states of Bornu. Distressed, all but two of his men left him, and soon these two also deserted to become the chiefs of Kanuri and Bagirmi. Because he could no longer enjoy the confidence of the people of Bornu he took his wife, the daughter of the king of Bornu, to Minan in Bamagaran. While in Minan a son named Biram was born to him. From Minan he proceeded to Daura, arriving there late in the day, and being thirsty he begged for drinking water, only to be told that there was a shortage of water in the town. The shortage was blamed upon a snake that frightened people away from the well. The snake called Kii or Seriki was killed by Abayejidu. For a reward the queen gave him half the town to rule, but he wanted more than that. He wanted to marry the queen. Some people say that he married the princess. It is very likely that he married the queen because visitors to the place often referred to it as the house of Mai-kas-seriki, meaning 'the man who killed the snake'. Ever after the word *seriki* or *sarki* came to mean chieftain in Hausa.

In addition to the queen, Abayejidu had a concubine who bore him a son named by the queen Mun-karba-gari, meaning 'we have taken the town'. Eventually the queen gave birth to a son called Bawo-ma-gari, meaning 'give back the town'. The two women had seven children respectively, giving rise to the two Hausa groups – the Hausa Bokwoi and the Hausa Banza. The Hausa Bokwoi comprises Daura, Kano, Zauzau or Zaria, Gobir, Rano, Biram and Katsina. They descended from the queen and are regarded as the legitimate sons while the Hausa Banza or bastards descended from the concubine and comprise Kebbi, Nupe, Gwari, Yauri, Ilorin, Zamfara and Kwararafa.

It is clear that we cannot pinpoint the origin of the Hausa, but all that is certain is that by the end of the eighteenth century the Hausa States were in existence irrespective of who were their original founders. However, we can indulge in some reasonable speculation as to their origin. It has been suggested that Abu Yazid was probably the head of a Berber army which was defeated and driven out of North Africa during the Fatimid dynasty in the tenth century. In trying to answer the question as to who were the founders of the Hausa States, we have to examine events that were taking place in the Western Sudan as a whole during the medieval era. About the eighth century A.D. groups of nomads collectively known as the Zaghawa entered various parts of the Western Sudan from the east or north-east, and established themselves as ruling aristocracies in various places. In Waddai, east of Lake Chad, surviving descendants of the Zaghawa have been identified. The Zaghawa were interested in iron-working and there are to be found today in Hausaland castes of highly skilled metal-workers known by the name Zogoran or Zugurma, a name probably derived from Zaghawa. Probably it is a branch of the Zaghawa conquerors of the Western Sudan. The Zaghawa were Berbers and it is generally known that Berbers of the southern Sahara throughout medieval times descended upon the tribes living in the region of Lake Chad. The fertile country of Hausaland would be attractive to nomads from the less favoured Sahara. The Hausa language itself is believed to show signs of strong Berber influence.

What Hausa traditions of origin represent as happening in one generation may well have taken a century or more. It seems quite clear that the Hausa States were established at different times, possibly separated by long intervals. The Hausa Banza states probably represent a later extension of Berber domination of the large region generally known as Hausaland.

We do not have as much documentation as we would like in order to write the history of the Hausa States, but these facts must be borne in mind, namely, that the states were pagan before the thirteenth century A.D., by which time Islam probably penetrated Hausaland. Each state was named after its principal city; it was often surrounded by mud walls and deep ditches which afforded security against enemy invasion; and each was independent of the others. Inter-state wars were not uncommon, but the common enemy fostered collective defence. The constant internecine wars weakened the states, and as a result no one state was able to dominate the others. This fact also lessened their effectiveness in defence of the common interest. Naturally such a situation among a heterogeneous stock resulted in stagnation.

Every state, however, had a specific duty to perform in the interests of the others. Gobir was on the edge of the desert and acted as a watch-dog against the Tuareg invaders. To the south was Zaria that acted as the slave-dealer with the forest traders. Rano was an industrial centre while Kano and Katsina were the emporium.

Individually the states did not exercise equal influence upon Hausaland. Three among them are therefore worthy of mention for the part they played in the early history of the Hausa. The states are Zaria, Katsina and Kano.

Zaria

To the Hausa people it was known as Zazzau, but non-Hausas called it Zagzag or Zegzeg. The capital of the state rotated from place to place until the present city which, according to most historians, was founded in the first half of the sixteenth century by Queen Bakwa Turuuku. The queen called the city by her daughter's name, and that accounts for assigning the founding of present Zaria to Amina or Aminamu. Aminamu was a very powerful princess who secured the city against invasion by building strong walls around it. So powerful was she that tributes were paid her by Kano and Katsina people. During her reign the state was extended to include Bauchi and beyond. It is said that 'her possessions stretched down to the shores of the sea'. Zaria suffered the same fate with the other six states when in 1734 Bornu invaded the Hausa States and Zaria began to pay tribute to Bornu. As a subject state, her kings were crowned by the king of Bornu or his representative. The next defeat was at the hands of the Fulani, but in this case the king removed his headquarters to Abuja. Not only was Zaria commercially important, but it also acted as a meeting place for the slave dealers of Katsina and Kano. The latter sold its slaves to the Arabs. In that way there was a diffusion of culture between the forest tribes, the Hausa and East African peoples. When in A.D. 1456 Islam penetrated Zaria, the path of invasion followed the slave trade troute.

Katsina

It will be observed that Katsina is among the original names of the Hausa Bokwoi and emerged as one of the influential states in Northern Nigeria. Its existence lends weight to the suggestion that Hausaland was occupied long before the arrival of the foreigners (the Hausa) into the land, and that the people of Katsina may have been the descendants of the original owners of the land. To link the state with the Hausa, however, a tradition associates Kumayo, one of the sons of Bawo, with the founding of Katsina. This, it is said, he achieved by conquest. Traditionally Janzama was the first king of the Katsina people on the arrival of the eastern migrants whose leader, Kumayo, fought and defeated and named the city after his wife, Katsina.

From the sixteenth century until the middle of the eighteenth century Hausaland suffered a number of invasions, first by Songhai, then by the

Kwararafawa followed by Bornu. After these invasions Katsina emerged as the leading Hausa state. During the eighteenth century Katsina was certainly the chief city in Hausaland. After the towns of Mali and Songhai to the west declined after the Moroccan invasion, Katsina developed into a great centre of the trans-Saharan trade. It became prosperous through trade and attracted considerable numbers of foreigners. Several wards or sections of the city still bear the names of the particular groups of foreign nationals who lived there, such as Songhai, Mali, Ashen and Bornu.

Already in the eighteenth century Katsina was becoming an important centre of Moslem learning to which students from far and near converged. Henry Barth, who visited Katsina in 1851, well attested the pre-eminent position of the city. Barth considered that 'Katsina during the seventeenth and eighteenth centuries ... seems to have been the chief city of ... Negroland, and as well in commercial and political importance as other respects'. Barth attributed the state of civilization that had been gradually built up in Katsina largely to contact with Arabs. This contact followed the development of the city as an important terminus of the caravan route that carried the trans-Saharan trade into Hausaland and the region of Lake Chad.

The Fulani revolt in Hausaland which started in the first decade of the nineteenth century brought to an end the prosperity and pre-eminence of Katsina. The city began to decline rather quickly. Its merchants moved out to Kano which now began to gain some of the glory and prestige of its former rival city.

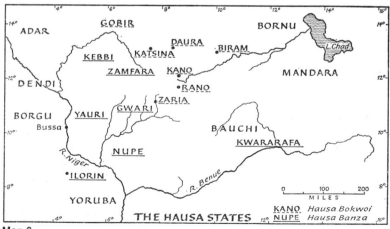

Map 6

Kano

The information we have on Kano comes from the *Kano Chronicle* which lists, from Bagoda to Bello, forty-eight kings. Bagoda, who was the son of Bawo, links the city of Kano to the Hausa Bokwoi. The earlier inhabitants, known as the Abagayawa, were blacksmiths who worked in iron-stone. Yet the *Kano Chronicle* maintains that the earliest ruler of Kano was a giant of a man who was in the habit of killing elephants with a mere walking-stick, and carrying them home single-handed. The man who made Kano famous was Mohammed Rimfa (1463–99). He built new walls around the city to replace those that were built in the twelfth century, encouraged Islamic missionaries, built mosques, caused sacred groves to be cut down, established the custom of the seclusion of women, and gave the lead in the observation of old prayers. However, before his time, camels had been introduced to Kano, and with these beasts of burden, the trade in salt became an important item of merchandise. After the death of Rimfa, Islam was corrupted by pagan elements and ceased to expand, but the faith was reactivated at the beginning of 1804.

Militarily Kano was unimportant, but commercially it was unrivalled by any of the Hausa States. Slaves from Zaria were in the main deposited in the famous Kano Market, to which even traders from the Middle East flocked. It was, and still is, the wealthiest emirate in Northern Nigeria. Kano captured the imagination of travellers and writers, and one can safely say that it placed Northern Nigeria on the map of the Sudan.

The conquest of the Hausa States

The Fulani *Jihad* of 1804 was not the only war that the Hausas fought to protect themselves and their land. On the contrary, there had been several occasions on which the Hausa people suffered defeat or temporary set-back at the hands of invaders. We shall now consider the two most important invasions. Among the major wars was that of 1504 following the return of Askia of Songhai from Mecca. In that year he destroyed the Baribas of Dahomey, and the following year, 1505, he attacked the Mandingoes. He next allied with Kanta, King of Kebbi, by whose help he entered Hausaland. The first victim was the state of Gobir, followed by Katsina and Zaria. Kano put up a gallant fight but fell after a long and protracted siege. Thus Hausaland came under the Songhai empire. However, this was not for long, because Askia's one-time ally, Kanta, the king of Kebbi, fought and defeated him, and became, as a result, the master of some Hausa provinces.

Another set-back to the progress and stability of the Hausa states was Bornu. Under its able king Mai Idris Alooma (1571–1603?), Bornu saddled the Habe with constant war. His energy was directed mainly upon Kano whose strong wall offered a strong defence. Similarly the Kwararafa, beginning in the fourteenth century, launched an attack from the south upon the Hausas. They invaded Bauchi and Zaria, and it seems they were not altogether successful, but before the end of the sixteenth century they renewed the attack by advancing on Kano. Once Kano was taken, the surrounding provinces fell easy prey. Thus a greater portion of Hausaland came under the Jukun empire of Kwararafa. The last and most crushing defeat suffered by the Hausa States at the hands of Africans began in 1804. This was the famed *jihad* of Usman dan Fodio with which we shall now deal.

The arrival of Islam in Hausaland and the Fulani *Jihad*
It has been said earlier on that the Habes were originally pagan, just as many states in the forest belt were pagan before the coming of Christianity. The precise date of the coming of Islam into Hausaland is not known, but some say it was during the thirteenth century A.D. Islam first reached Hausaland from the west through the agency of Wangara traders from Mali. These traders began to penetrate Hausaland in the late twelfth and early thirteenth centuries; but it was not until well into the fourteenth century that the Islamic faith gained a footing in Hausaland.

Islam was introduced into Kano, according to the *Kano Chronicle*, by Wangara teachers brought into the town by King Yedzi (1349–85). By the fifteenth century Islam had reached Zaria, the most southerly Hausa state. With the conquest of Gobir and Kebbi by Songhai, Islam was forced on some of the Hausa.

The history of Islam in Hausaland proper must be traced to the Fulani. These people entered Northern Nigeria in small pockets, and one of the important groups came from the direction of Mali, establishing themselves in Sokoto while others settled in Bornu, Adamawa and Gobir. The date of their entry is put as A.D. 1400. For the next four centuries the Fulani Moslems quietly and unobstrusively infiltrated the Hausa society, and had long before the *jihad* secured administrative offices in Zaria and other states.

The spread of Islam in Hausaland was aided by the rise of Uthman Ibn Muhammad Ibn Fudi, otherwise known as Usman dan Fodio (1754–1817). He descended from the Torodbe section of the Fulani who settled in Gobir. Born in Islamic faith, he was influenced by an orthodox Moslem teacher, Jibril Ibn Umar, and therefore recoiled from the admixture of Islam and pagan practices within the society.

It would appear that Islam was not making much impact upon heathenism and the malams seemed helpless in the face of pagan practices. To purify Islam and make it a dynamic force in the society Usman organized an order of preachers into wandering preachers. From 1774 to 1775 he was In the vanguard of preachers to evangelize Gobir. He was later (1781) engaged by Bawa Jangworzo, the Sarkin of Gobir, as a tutor to the royal family because of his learning in Islamic law and theology. While in the royal court he was shocked by the abuse of Islam among the Hausa nobility.

Parting with royalty in 1786, Usman once more entered upon a wider field of evangelism that embraced Zamfara and nearby states. To check the religious exuberance, Sarkin Gobir decreed that only those born Moslems should be permitted to practise Islam. The decree was a counterblast to further conversions. He further decreed against the wearing of turbans. However, what sparked off open hostilities was the release by Usman of certain Moslem followers who had been taken captive In war. Sarkin Yunfa, who had ascended the throne in 1802, invaded the little village of Degel where Usman lived. His flight, on 21 February 1804, to Gudu was an important turning point. There a stop was made while Abdullahi, his brother, fought and defeated Yunfa's army. Following the battle, Usman's followers launched the *jihad* and proclaimed him Sarkin Musulmi or chief of the Moslems – a title which Askia of Songhai had held, and which is still held by the Sultan of Sokoto.

Frightened by the unexpected defeat of his army, Yunfa warned other emirs of the Hausa states against annihilation by Usman. Attacks on Usman's followers in the different states united the Fulani against the common enemy – the Hausas – and in retaliation Usman commissioned his leading followers with flags to proclaim the *jihad*. An attempt by the Hausas at a united attack failed and consequently by 1810 the Fulani hegemony was established over the Hausa States. For example, Zaria was defeated in 1805, Katsina in 1807, Gobir in 1808, and Kano in 1809. Nor was the conquest limited to the Hausa States. Many non-Hausa states were subjected to Fulani rule except the present Plateau Province, the Jukun, Tiv and Idoma, south of the Benue, and part of Kabba and Ilorin in Yoruba country.

Organizing the vast territory was difficult for one man and so the Shehu partitioned it between his son, Bello, and his brother, Abdullahi. Bello ruled the eastern half with headquarters at Sokoto, comprising the original Hausa States down to the Benue at Nasarawa, Muri and Yola. Abdullahi ruled the western half from a point a hundred miles south- west of Sokoto, stretching to the River Niger and including the Nupe kingdom and, later, Ilorin in Yoruba country. The capital of the new emirate was Gwandu. Eventually it was changed to Birnin Kebbi. All along, the descendants of Abdullahi have occupied the throne. For example, the President of the former Northern House of Chiefs, Alhaji Haruna, CMG, CBE, is a direct descendant of Abdullahi and cousin of the late Northern Premier, Alhaji Ahmadu Bello, the Sardauna of Sokoto.

Much as the Hausa States were disunited and their belated united front against a common foe proved abortive, it must be observed that Usman served as a God-sent person for the oppressed Hausas who were seeking redress from oppressive taxation and economic exploita- tion. It may also be noted that long before the *jihad*, Islam had made an inroad among the society, and that part of the Islamic doctrine which stated that the function of a state was to provide proper conditions for the good life of the citizens was not forgotten by the oppressed. It implied that where such proper condition was not provided, the citizens could revolt.

Once in power, however, the conquerors lost sight of the original aim of the *jihad*, namely to improve the society and purify Islam by purging it of foreign and pagan practices. Sokoto, for example, became the recip- ient of tributes in slaves, money and cloth from all over the conquered territories. Administratively, original state boundaries were altered, and while the broad government machinery was based on Islam, the structure was Hausa. The rulers adopted Hausa titles as, for example, Zaki ('lion') or Sarkin, which now denoted 'chief' or 'ruler'. To reward the flag-bearers Usman appointed them fief-holders over a specified ter- ritory. This territory eventually became an emirate with an emir as the executive head. While each ruler was independent, allegiance was paid by all to the Shehu, and Sokoto was looked upon as the spiritual centre and political headquarters of the empire.

Following the death of Usman dan Fodio in 1817, Bello became the Sarkin Musulmi, some say by a *coup*. Soon after the people of Gwandu had staged an unsuccessful *coup*, Bello and Abdullahi met and healed the rift as the latter, in traditional Muslim etiquette, greeted Bello as the Commander of the Faithful. By this simple act the two men demon- strated their obedience to leadership that characterizes the Hausas of Nigeria. Bello was succeeded in 1837 not by his son, Said, but his brother, Abu Bakr, with the attendant result of palace intrigues and squabbles which robbed the *jihad* of complete success. Ali reigned from 1842 to 1859 and during this period the empire began to encounter great difficulties. Provincial governors began to assert their own authority and this state of affairs continued until 1904 when the British attacked and took Sokoto, killing At-Tahir, the ruler.

Part Two: The Southern Forest Region

8 States of the forest belt: Oyo, Benin, Dahomey

The land and peoples

The vast area of West Africa lying between the grasslands of the Western Sudan and the Gulf of Guinea is generally regarded as a forest belt. The heart of this southern region is thick equatorial forest, and some of it is almost impenetrable mangrove forest. However, there are fairly extensive stretches of land in this area which are really not forested. Cocoa and coffee plantations have in recent years been responsible for the thinning of the forest in many places. This is especially so in Ghana, Western Nigeria and the Ivory Coast.

The Niger and the Volta are the most prominent rivers. The former affords a valuable waterway while the latter is navigable for only small craft for just over seventy miles inland from the sea. As at its great bend in the north, the Niger at its approaches to the Bight of Benin in the south has always attracted concentrated populations. In what may be called southern Nigeria today the river has along its banks some of the most virile groups of people in Africa.

We have observed that the southern region of West Africa is not entirely forested. Some of the states to be dealt with in this region arose in areas where in modern times there has been virtually no forest. Dahomey is one such example. Oyo also was on the fringe of the rain forest and based its power in Western Yorubaland on cavalry as much as the more northerly states did. In the truly forested areas of the region the nature of the land influenced historical developments. While the open nature of the Western Sudan facilitated movement, in the south the forest was, generally speaking, a serious hindrance to movement. It was in many respects a barrier to the movement of men and subsequently of ideas. While the ambitious state-builder of the Western Sudan could spread conquest and domination far and wide in a short space of time, his counterpart in the southern forest had to beat his way slowly and wearily through undergrowth in difficult country. The horse, which gave the warrior statesman of the savanna mobility and served his empire-building schemes, could hardly serve the warrior chief of the forest, owing to the prevalence of the tsetse-fly. The limitations on movement and military campaigns necessarily made most of the states of the rain forest smaller than the medieval kingdoms and empires of the Western Sudan. Some of the states in the properly forested areas such as those in Ibo country developed political institutions that were always typically on the village level while some of the states of the Niger delta, although small, were city states based very firmly on overseas trade.

On the whole, important and powerful states did flourish with astonishing vitality in the southern region of West Africa. The states of the south were in many ways more coherent, more closely knit together, than those of the Western Sudan.

The vitality of the states of the southern region, whether great or small, was largely due to the nature of the Negro of the south. Although akin to the Negro of the Western Sudan, the inhabitants of the southern region are generally a sturdy, stocky and vivacious race. The true Negro is really to be found in the southern region. Robust and resourceful, the Negro of the south are quick to learn and adapt, and they have displayed amazing skill in political organization. They developed great confidence in themselves. The riverain dwellers of the Niger delta established very stable city states. The Dahomeyans on the coast commanded armies of both men and women and compelled the respect of the White traders on that part of the West African coast, and their movements and activities were placed under careful control. The Yoruba of Nigeria impressed outsiders with their amazing skill in handicraft and their gift for statesmanship. The Asante, confident in their valour and knowledge of forest warfare, could boast and make fun of a British expeditionary force, saying: 'the White Man brings his cannon to the forest but the forest proves too strong for him'. One invading Asante king, on reaching the coast under the protection of the European, waded into the foaming sea and claimed to be *Bonsu* (the whale), lord of the sea.

To mention the Yoruba, Dahomeyans and the Asante is to select only the most prominent of the southern peoples. There are many more, some of whom have not yet claimed the full attention of the historian but who were by no means less brave and skilful in their contribution to the unwritten history of West Africa. In this book only the most prominent states of the southern region of West Africa can be considered.

Some of the peoples of the southern region of West Africa must have been living in their present homes since early times. Such old inhabitants appear to have fallen prey at one time or the other to incoming waves of people more warlike and more skilful than themselves. Today it is practically impossible to distinguish with any degree of certainty the descendants of the vanquished from those of the victors. Both have been welded together into common units of people. The conquering groups often bestowed upon the conquered peoples their superior skills of fighting and statecraft, while the latter would influence the former with their language. The inferior numbers of the conquering tribes would force them to adopt the languages of the conquered tribes. Intermarriage stamped upon both groups a common fate and development. The southern region was invaded in early times by small groups of people from the northern grasslands. A mass movement of the peoples from north to south appears improbable. Traders, missionaries and adventurers crossed from savanna to forest and back again from early times.

External influences
We have seen during the course of the history of the Western Sudan that there is some obscurity surrounding the origins of the medieval states and kingdoms of the savanna. The history of the origins of the states of the southern region of West Africa is even more obscure. Fragmentary as the origins of the Western Sudanese states are, the records left by Arabic scholars and travellers supply important landmarks in the history of the Western Sudan. It has been possible to date some important events with considerable accuracy. The trans-Saharan caravan routes introduced the Western Sudan to the outside world very early, even if in a somewhat legendary way. In time also Western Sudanese historians and writers took to recording important events in the history of the Western Sudanese states. Literacy became open to Western Sudanese peoples at an early period.

Civilizing influences from the Mediterranean World coming into the Western Sudan have already been mentioned. The Western Sudan came into the limelight of world history in the early medieval period. However, the story of the states of the southern region presents a different picture. Moreover, hardly any of them possessed any written history until quite recent times. The result of this handicap is that much of the early history of the peoples of the southern region has had to be pieced together out of tradition. Archaeology has yet to confirm a good deal of what has been glimpsed through local traditions. Our knowledge of the early and medieval history of the southern region is therefore limited.

It is true that the interior of the southern region of West Africa remained for many years closed to outsiders. By the end of the fifteenth century the outline of the entire coast of West Africa had become known to Europeans and trade with Africans had begun on a considerable scale. But for centuries the Europeans hardly ventured beyond their forts and castles. Europeans had traded on the Niger delta for three hundred years before they got to know that it was the same Niger that flowed through the Western Sudan.

The interior of the southern region of West Africa remained 'dark' for centuries. The seclusion of this vast and rich area has been attributed to various factors. In the first place the few big rivers flowing from north to south are only navigable over short stretches. The impenetrable mangrove forest has always had its share of responsibility for the darkness of the interior, and so has the hostility of the tribes of the region. The inability of Europeans to survive in the humid equatorial climate has often been stressed as another great hindrance to penetration into the interior from the coast. All these factors more or less contributed to the interior of the southern region remaining obscure for many generations. However, the seclusion of the states of this part of West Africa should not be exaggerated. Such exaggeration as has been made is largely the result of ignorance of the early history of these states.

There are clear indications that the peoples of the southern region were exposed at various periods in their early history to outside influence. They learned useful lessons from outside, although it is not easy now to determine the extent and real nature of these lessons. The Negroes of the southern region certainly received influences from beyond their territories.

There are persistent traditions of outside origins for nearly all the prominent states of the south. The Yoruba who built the Oyo empire have strong traditions of eastern origins. The Akan of modern Ghana point to an ancestral home somewhere in the northern grasslands. Just as the rigours of journeying across the Sahara did not deter brave travellers from the Mediterranean coast from crossing into the Western Sudan, so also even the thick forests did not deter the intrepid Sudanese trader and traveller from venturing south. It must be remembered that the forest and the Western Sudan are separately by a considerable depth of light bush in which movement is not very difficult. The quest for valuable commodities has throughout human history defied the most difficult of geographical barriers. In old times the forest held articles much sought after by traders from the Western Sudan. Gold, kola and slaves were taken from areas of the southern region into the Western Sudan and beyond. The Hausa States obtained many slaves from the south. The old capital of Oyo in Yorubaland was linked to Hausaland by trade routes. Mande-speaking traders from the Western Sudan are known to have made regular journeys southward into Asante. Asante gold is believed to have found its way to North Africa by way of the Western Sudan. In Gyaman territory north-west of Asante in the Republic of Ghana can be seen the ruins of an old Mande settlement called Begho. It is now known that Mande-speaking people arrived in Begho long before the rise of the kingdom of Asante. Begho was in fact an important stopping place on a trade route between the south and the Western Sudan. The northern terminus of the trade route was Jenne. 'Begho became an outpost of the civilization of the Middle Niger, a colony of Mande-speaking peoples thrust out to the very fringes of the rich gold-bearing and kola-producing forest country, a collecting point not only for the gold from its immediate locality, but for that and the other products of the forest to the south'.*

The state of Gonja in the Republic of Ghana to the far north-west of Asante is known to have been founded in about the first half of the seventeenth century. Ties between the Nigerian end of the southern region and the savannaland to the north appear to have been equally strong. There seems to have been an appreciable commercial link between Hausaland and Yorubaland. The Rev. Samuel Johnson writing on the history of the Yoruba has said: 'Light and civilization with the Yorubas came from the north; the centres of life and activity of large populations and industry were in the interior'. There is no doubt that almost throughout the length and breadth of the southern region of West Africa there was considerable contact with the grasslands to the north. The peoples of the south must have come under some cultural and political influences from the Western Sudan as a result of the contact.

The Oyo empire of the Yoruba

Origin of the Yoruba
The land covering the Western Region of the Federal Republic of Nigeria

* Ivor Wilks, *The Northern Factor in Ashanti History,* Institute of African Studies, University of Ghana, 1961, p. 7.

and stretching westward to Dahomey was, in the later Middle Ages and after, the scene of a number of states, great and small, controlled by the Yoruba-speaking people. It has even been claimed that at one time the vast area from the banks of the Niger to the Volta had come under the authority of Yoruba rulers. Of the several Yoruba kingdoms Oyo remained dominant for centuries (Map 7).

The main guide to the early history of Yoruba is oral tradition. The shortcomings of this source of history have been mentioned already in this book. The Yoruba claim that their ancestors entered Nigeria after migrating from the north or north-east. Some of the traditions specifically point to Mecca as the home of origin, but it is suspected that this is mainly due to Islamic influence. Yoruba origins are embodied in a legend rather like that of the Hausa States of the north. The name of the much-revered legendary ancestral hero of the Yoruba is Oduduwa. He is portrayed in several variants of the legend as an eastern prince who, driven out of his kingdom in the east, finally entered Nigeria after a long march with his followers. After successful battles fought against the local population, Oduduwa and his people finally settled down at Ife. Oduduwa had seven children and eventualy these or their own children became the founders of seven Yoruba kingdoms. The seven children of Oduduwa became the Olowu of Owu, the Onisabe of Sabe, the Olupopo of Popo, the Oba of Benin, the ruler of Illa, the Alaketu of Ketu and last but not the least the Alafin of Oyo.

It is quite certain that whatever their origin the Yoruba made their first main settlement at Ife. Probably the founding of Ife took place towards the end of the first millenium. From Ife new settlements and conquests were made by the Yoruba. Ife, where Oduduwa first established a firm foothold in Nigeria, gave way in political importance to Oyo but remained the ancestral and spiritual home of all the Yoruba. The Oni of Ife, as the ruler of Ife is called, has always been regarded as the spiritual head of the Yoruba. On the coronation of the Alafin of Oyo and of the rulers of the other Yoruba states the sword of state had to be brought from Ife for the ceremony.

The legend of Oduduwa and his seven sons seems to be a simplified remembered version of a complex chain of events of conquest and formation of kingdoms and states in what became Yorubaland. If we are to consider the main part of the tradition of origin which points to an ancestral home in the east or north-east, we could say it all started with a movement from 'somewhere' in the east or north-east into the forest country of Nigeria. A small group, or most probably groups, of people

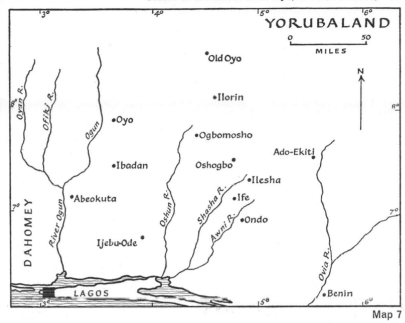

Map 7

from the east or north-east may have made their way into Nigeria under adventurous leaders, one of whom is remembered as Oduduwa. Whether the Yoruba migration was by means of an armed invasion or peaceful penetration, the several political units or states that emerged must have taken generations to form. The eastern invaders were in all likelihood outnumbered by the local people. We thus see in Yorubaland the same incidence of 'invasion' and fusion already discussed in connection with the kingdoms and states of the Western Sudan.

One point ought to be stressed – the invasion of Yorubaland by groups of people from the east or north-east should not be regarded as necessarily the act of civilized people against uncivilized aborigines. If the eastern invaders supplied the political skill and impetus necessary for the building of strong kingdoms, the local peoples also had a good deal to offer to the new political units culturally. The invasion of Yoruba-land by the people from the east is believed to have taken place about a thousand years ago – between A.D. 700 and 1000. It appears that local people were already farmers and iron and bronze-workers. The tradi-tion of metalwork in Nigeria, both north and south, goes back to ancient times. For example, the great civilization of the Benue region known as Nok culture pre-dates the migration of the ancestors of the Yoruba into

Nigeria by centuries. It is interesting to recall that after the fall of Mero in the Nile valley in about A.D. 350, some of the skilled iron-workers of the city fled westward. It is possible that in this way the knowledge of Meroic metal work spread westwards until it reached Nigeria. It may well be also that metalwork as an ancient craft penetrated into the southern forest of Nigeria in very early times from the north-east, possibly from Egypt or Nubia.

Oyo

The origins of Oyo are not clear. Again we are beset by variants of a legend. One Yoruba tradition, which is incidentally colaborated by Benin tradition, has it that Oduduwa, the legendary founding father of Yoruba, sent out a son or grandson called Oranmiyan to rule over Benin. According to Benin tradition the Bini had sent to Ife for a prince of royal blood to become king of Benin. In any case, finding the people of Benin rather troublesome, Oranmiyan decided to abdicate in favour of a son born to him by a Bini woman. Oranmiyan himself retired north and set up a new capital for himself at Old Oyo (also known as Katunga) some eighty miles north of the present Yoruba town of Oyo. Whether Oranmiyan was only a legendary or a real historical figure we may never know. What is important, however, is that he represents a stage in the development of Yoruba influence and power in Nigeria. It is interesting that Oranmiyan should be linked in common ancestry with the dynasties of the two most powerful states of southern Nigeria – Oyo and Benin. Oranmiyan represents the stage of Yoruba history in which Oyo replaces Ife as the centre of political power. Historians have tentatively dated this period between 1388 and 1431. The present Alafin of Oyo is said to be forty-third in direct line of succession to Oranmiyan, founder of Oyo, or whoever it was. It would be reasonable on such reckoning to say that Oyo was probably founded about 1400.

Another variant of the legend of Yoruba origin says that it was Oranyam, one of the seven sons of Oduduwa, who became the first king or Alafin of Oyo. Be that as it may, until 1837, when the site of the capital was moved farther south to the present town of Oyo, Katunga or Old Oyo remained the centre of a vast empire which at its peak was bounded to the north by the Niger, to the east by Benin, to the west by the frontier of modern Togo and to the south by the mangrove swamps and lagoons. The king or Alafin of Oyo was in fact an emperor with a number of provincial kings under him. The nature of relationship between the Alafin and the provinces was determined by a number of factors, including the distance from the capital of Oyo of a particular province, the personality and strength of the provincial rulers, and the effectiveness of the Alafin's government in Oyo itself. The Alafin's authority appears to have been generally felt only in Oyo province proper, an area extending about 100 miles from north to south and 150 miles from east to west. The remoter provinces were virtually independent. For example, Ekiti just north of Oyo proper and Ijebu to the south-east remained independent for practical purposes.

The early Alafins

It is no easy task to try to summarize coherently the reigns of the early Alafins of Oyo. Oyo was founded probably about A.D. 1400. The present Alafin, as already pointed out, is said to be the forty-third in direct line of succession from Oranmiyan, founder of Oyo. Oranmiyan was

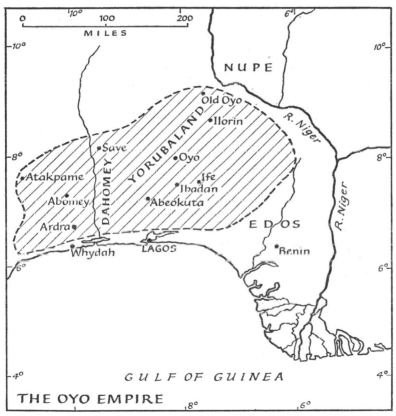

Map 8

succeeded by his son, Ajaka, who appears to have been a mild or even weak ruler. He was unable to keep his father's territories under control and was in the end deposed by his people. Ajaka was succeeded by Sango, who was not only a strong ruler but also a very notable magician. In a magical feat one day Sango is said to have directed lightning inadvertently unto his own household, killing many of his wives and children. He hanged himself after the incident but was deified as the God of Thunder and Lightning. The cult or worship of Sango or Shango is practised throughout Yorubaland and Benin as well as in Dahomey to the west. This popularity of the worship of Sango may be taken as a pointer to the wide influence of Oyo.

After Sango had destroyed himself, Ajaka managed to be reinstated as Alafin and this time showed himself as an active ruler. He conducted successful battles against the Nupe people living immediately to the north-east of Oyo Province. From Oranmiyan to Ajaka a good deal of what we are told concerning the activities of the monarchs of Oyo belongs to the realm of myth so that it is difficult to assess the truth of it. However, from the first half of the sixteenth century we enter the period of reasonably historical events with the accession of Onigboni as Alafin of Oyo. In Onigboni's reign the Nupe invaded Yorubaland and succeeded in destroying the capital, Old Oyo. An independent study of the Nupe people confirms this event and gives an indication of the period as being during the first half of the sixteenth century. Onigboni's successor, Ofonran, defeated and drove back the Nupe from Yorubaland but died while still leading his people back to the capital from exile. It was left to Ofonran's successor, Egugoujo, to lead back the Yoruba to Old Oyo. On his arrival Egugoujo found the old capital almost in ruins and decided to establish a new and probably temporary capital at Oyo Igboho. Four Alafins reigned at Oyo Igboho. This was a stormy period in the history of Oyo filled with almost continuous wars against both the Nupe and Bussa people. The Alafin Abipa moved the capital back to Old Oyo where it remained until it was abandoned in 1837.

Ojigi, the ninth Alafin to reign in Old Oyo after the return from exile, effected a healthy revival in the fortunes of the kingdom. With Ojigi we enter a new phase of the history of Oyo in which facts and dates become more certain. Ojigi is credited with a positive drive for territorial expansion during which Oyo armies made war on Dahomey and attacked Porto Novo in 1698. He started a war against the young kingdom of Dahomey by attacking the state of Great Ardra, which Dahomey had been aspiring to control. Ojigi's men waged a ruthless war. A description of the exploits of the Oyo fighters states that they used horses and quickly overran the territories of Ardra. They slaughtered such large numbers of the enemy that in expressing the figures of the dead it was commonly reported – 'They were like the grains of corn in the field'.*

The first half of the eighteenth century witnessed further victories by Oyo armies against Dahomey. In 1724 Dahomey defied the authority of the Alafin of Oyo and invaded Great Ardra in the hope of gaining an access to the sea. The Alafin quickly despatched an army against Dahomey. The Dahomeyans in the end sued for peace and sent presents to the Alafin as a sign of submission. But three years later in 1727 Dahomey started a fresh effort to gain access to the sea, this time by invading Whydah. In response to an appeal for help by Whydah the Alafin sent a large army against Dahomey. The Yorubas laid waste many Dahomeyan villages. In 1729 Dahomey again sued for peace and agreed to pay tribute to Oyo. In 1738 armies of Oyo attacked Dahomey, for the king of Dahomey would not pay to the Alafin the tribute imposed in 1729. The Oyo army laid siege to Abomey, the capital of Dahomey. When Dahomey finally asked for peace Oyo demanded the following tribute: '40 men, 40 women, 40 guns and 400 loads of cowries and corals a year to date with effect from the defeat of 1728'.† Dahomey defaulted for a number of years but finally submitted to the terms after threats of fresh invasion by Oyo.

Political organization

The political organization of the kingdom of Oyo was quite complex. The Alafin was elected from among a number of royal candidates by a king-making body called the *Oyo Mesi* composed of seven councillors of state. It is interesting to note that the Alafin's eldest son, known by the title of Aremo, could not be elected to succeed to his father's post. The Aremo, moreover, had to commit suicide on the announcement of the Alafin's death. When an Alafin displeased his people he was presented with an empty calabash or parrot's eggs as a sign that he must commit suicide.

The Alafin was surrounded by a number of title-holders in his court but it was the Oyo Mesi who controlled policy of state. One member of the Mesi, known as the Basorum, held the position of a Prime Minister. If an unsatisfactory Alafin had to die by the wish of his people, it was the Basorum who communicated the fact to the Alafin. No doubt the

* E. G. Parrinder, *The Story of Ketu,* Ibadan University Press, 1956, p. 26.
† In the same work, p. 28.

D

Basorum was in the position to determine or influence such a decision. The Basorum declared to the Alafin: 'The Gods reject you, the people reject you, the earth rejects you'. As a check against the power of both the Alafin and the Oyo Mesi stood a secret society called the Ogboni. The members of the society were drawn from religious and political leaders. They had direct access to the Alafin and it was their special responsibility to try cases of bloodshed, an offence regarded as abominable to the earth. The Ogboni moreover had the right to review and even reject certain decisions of the Oyo Mesi. It is clear that although a strong Alafin could exercise great authority in his own right, by and large, the post of Alafin by itself did not confer absolute rule on the holder. The Alafin's authority was restricted by checks and balances in the political organization of Oyo.

Next in importance to the Oyo Mesi ranked the Esos. They were the guardians of the kingdom and were also known by the military title of *Iba*. The greatest among the Esos was the Kakanfo, who was in fact the commander of the Oyo army. A Kakanfo who led an unsuccessful expedition or lost an important battle had to commit suicide.

The provinces and towns under Oyo were headed by local chiefs known as the Oba.

The rise and fall of the Oyo empire

The Oyo empire broke up in the course of the nineteenth century. By then the Oyo kingdom of the Yoruba had held sway for about five hundred years. The remarkable success of Oyo can be attributed to several factors. The first and foremost of these factors was the efficient army maintained by Oyo. This army was responsible not only for imperial expansion but also for keeping the dissident elements within the empire quiet. The exploits of the Oyo army in Dahomey have already been alluded to. During the imperial period Oyo actually encouraged the development of a class of professional war chiefs.

Reference has already been made to the area within immediate control of Oyo – Yoruba Proper, as this may be called. This area was the core and the source of strength of the Oyo empire. Bound together by ties of kinship, common language and religion, Yoruba Proper provided a rare solidarity, which was the force behind the extensive empire that Oyo controlled. The third factor of success was the highly organized nature of the empire. We have already briefly reviewed the details of this organization. This well-organized political system was placed at the disposal of Alafins who were personally equal to the task of building and ruling an empire. The fact, also, that the Alafins enjoyed some sort of divinity raised their prestige among the provincial governors. Lastly there was the financial factor. The Oyo government had considerable wealth at its disposal. This wealth was mainly derived from tribute. It has been estimated that Dahomey alone paid to Oyo annual tribute to the tune of some £32,000. The Oyo government in addition derived financial benefits from trade with the north and, especially from the seventeenth century, from trade with the Europeans on the coast.

History teaches us that while still at the peak of power and glory empires and kingdoms may already hold the seeds of imminent decline and eventual fall. The Oyo victories over Dahomey during the first half of the eighteenth century certainly strengthened the authority of Oyo in a wide area to the west. But even so, serious cracks were showing in the organization of the Oyo empire. The second half of the eighteenth century saw serious signs of decline. In the nineteenth century the Oyo empire disintegrated leaving only Yoruba Proper to the authority of the Alafin.

At the time of the subjection of Dahomey the newly elected Alafin, Labisi, appointed one Gaha as Basorum. This proved to be an unfortunate appointment, for Gaha quickly killed at the court two men who were the chief supporters of the new Alafin, and in the end forced Labisi to commit suicide. Succeeding Alafins came increasingly under the control of Gaha. But when Abiodum became Alafin he plotted with the army commander, Kakanfo Oyabi, to get rid of the hateful Gaha. One day all the members of Gaha's family throughout the kingdom were seized and put to sudden death. The Basorum was himself arrested and burnt to death. The final overthrow of Gaha occurred in 1774. Thus Abiodum became the master of Oyo. But the horror of Gaha's destruction marked a turning point in the fortunes of the Oyo kingdom. Both secretly and openly resentment was expressed against the high-handed action by the Alafin.

King Adahoozu of Dahomey refused to pay the tribute imposed by Oyo. The province of Egba declared itself independent of the Alafin and succeeded in beating back an army sent against it by the Alafin. When Abiodum died in about March 1789 disintegration awaited the Oyo empire. The Rev. Samuel Johnson has left a gloomy account of this period of Oyo history. 'With Abiodum's death', Johnson writes, 'ended the universal and despotic rule of the Alafins of Oyo in the Yoruba country. He was the last of the kings who held the different parts of the kingdom together in one universal sway, and with him ended the tranquility and prosperity of the Yoruba country. The revolution came,

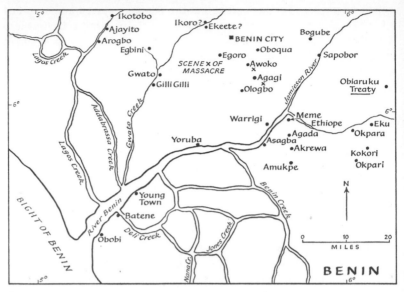

Map 9

resulting in the provinces of Tapa, Bariba and Dahomey regaining their independence from Oyo. In a word, with Abiodum ended the unity of the Yoruba kingdom'.

For one thing the administrative machine of the Oyo empire centred in the old capital and based on a balance of power between Alafin and Oyo Mesi in due course outlived its usefulness and became hardly serviceable to the administration of an expanding empire in changing conditions. The activities of Gaha, the Basorum, greatly discredited and weakened the central authority of Oyo. Another weakening factor was that the empire was over-stretched. This was particularly so in the absence of adequate means of communication between the Oyo capital and the provinces. The Oyo army itself, once the terror of neighbouring countries, began to lose its former fighting qualities until it became the shadow of its former self.

Economics had something to do with the decline of the Oyo empire. With the increasing development of trade on the coast following the appearance of the Europeans, especially from the seventeenth century, the south and not the north became the economic centre and focal point of trade and commerce, and consequently of power. However, Old Oyo was built most probably with an eye to the trans-Saharan trade; it looked to the north and not to the south. Now with the shift of the centre of economic activities and power, Old Oyo, looking to the north, could not adequately attend to its new interests in the south. The southern provinces of the empire began increasingly to cater for their own economic interests towards the coast, and hence were ready to seize any opportunity at hand to rid themselves of any control from Old Oyo. By the close of the eighteenth century many of the provincial rulers as well as the tributary states were anxious and ready to overthrow the authority of Oyo. This tendency was soon encouraged when at the beginning of the nineteenth century Kakanfo Afonja in Ilorin revolted against the authority of the Alafin. Afonja was helped by the Fulani, a situation which touched off civil wars throughout the Oyo empire. By 1824 only Yoruba Proper was left to the authority of the Alafin.

Benin

Origin and early history

According to Benin tradition, the people of Benin migrated from the east. After a long period of wandering they finally settled at Ile-Ife, from where Benin was scouted. What seems to be the first dynasty of Benin was founded by rulers known as 'Ogiso'. The leader who eventually emerged as the most outstanding was called Obagodo, during whose reign, it is said, there was great improvement in industry – woodcrafts, iron foundries and ceramics. After him reigned, according to tradition, ten monarchs, two among whom were women. The death of the last Ogiso was followed by an interregnum during which two men, Evian and Ogiamwe, acted as administrators. The land was then known as Igodomingodo (Map 9).

A semi legendary prince called Oranmiyan began what might be regarded as the second dynasty of Benin. Tradition says that, not satisfied with the administration of Evian and Ogiamwe during the interregnum, the people of Benin decided to make a return to the monarchy and subsequently sent to Ife for a prince of royal blood to rule over Benin. This is how local Benin tradition explains the appearance of the semi-legendary Oranmiyan of Ife in Benin. Perhaps Oranmiyan represents an invasion or domination of Benin by the Yoruba of Ife. It may be observed that local traditions have the tendency to make the inglorious past look less unpleasant. What local Benin tradition claims to have been an invitation to a prince of Ife to rule over Benin may be regarded as an attempt to water down the bitter fact of a Yoruba conquest. There is a revealing part of Benin tradition on this early period. Eweko, one of the early kings of the second dynasty, is said to have been debarred from entering Benin by Ogiamwe, son of one of the leaders of the interregnum of the same name. There was a great fight between Eweko and the younger Ogiamwe and the latter was finally defeated. It is worth noting that the victory of Eweko over Ogiamwe is still remembered and celebrated in the form of a mock battle at the coronation of a new Oba of Benin. This strengthens the suggestion of a Yoruba invasion of Benin leading to the second Benin dynasty.

It is said that Oranmiyan renounced his office as ruler of Benin on the grounds that Benin was 'a country of vexation'. He abdicated in favour of a son born to him by a woman of Benin. Oranmiyan moved northward to Oyo and it is said that he became the first Alafin of Oyo.

Eweka, the son of Oranmiyan, was eventually crowned as Oba Eweka I of Benin. His reign is said to have been a glorious one. He appointed his sons as dukes to various districts of his kingdom, and also created the office of king-makers or councillors of state. Their titles were made hereditary and it was they who crowned the obas. These king-makers were known as *Uzama-Nihinron.*

Eweka I was succeeded by his sons in turn, but the oba who appeared to have made his imprint upon Benin history was Ewedo, whose father was Oba Ehennihew, Eweka's son. Ewedo's reign was marked by innovations. He was interested in religion, and appointed his medicine-man the chief priest. He enacted laws, and built a central prison. He curtailed the power of the king-makers. For example, he stopped them from carrying swords of state like the oba. He is said to have changed the name of the country from Ife-Ibinu to Ubini. From the latter derived Benin.

During the reign of Ewedo's son, Oguola, the brass industry is said to have been introduced into Benin. After Oguola, six obas reigned without achieving much, but with the succession of Ewuare a new era began in Benin.

Ewuare the Great and his successors

Under Oba Ewuare, revered as Ewuare the Great, the authority of Benin extended far and wide. The new oba embarked upon an expansionist policy. Tradition has it that he conquered 201 towns and villages in Ekiti, Eka, Ikare, Kukuruku, and the Ibo country on the Asaba side of the River Niger. Ewuare was a remarkable man of many parts: he was a great magician and physician as well as a brave warrior. He combined warlike activities with initiating social developments. We are told that he built good roads to link all places in his empire.

Ewuare was the reigning oba when the first European, Ruy de Sequeira, visited Benin City in 1472. The various accounts show that Ruy de Sequiera and his Portuguese friends were favourably impressed with what they saw in Benin.

Following Ewuare's death, his eldest son made a brief appearance on the throne, and so did the second son, Olua. Olua was persuaded to become oba and was so crowned and he ruled until about 1481. The next oba, Ozolua, was as imperialistic as Ewuare and succeeded in incorporating into his empire neighbouring Yoruba towns. During his reign another Portuguese, John Alfonso d'Aveiro, visited Benin City in 1485–86 and trade was established. This man is said to have introduced guns and coconuts into Benin. John Alfonso d'Aveiro visited Benin for the second time in 1505 during the reign of Oba Esigie. The Portuguese sought pepper and slaves, but unhappily it was trade in the latter that predominated and ultimately contributed to the decline of Benin.

The attempt to introduce the Christian faith into Benin by the Portuguese was an important event in the reign of Esigie. Convinced by Alfonso, Oba Esigie sent Ohen-Okun from Gwatto as an ambassador to the court of Portugal, asking the king to send missionaries to teach him and his people the word of God. Not only did the king of Portugal send Roman Catholic priests to convert Oba Esigie and his people, but also gifts of a copper stool, coral beads and an umbrella. Commercial contacts were also established between the two kingdoms, and the port of Gwatto became an entrepôt of southern Nigeria. From it such goods as ivory, palm produce (oil and kernel), native cloths and pepper were exported. The missionary endeavours of the Portuguese, however, do not appear to have yielded encouraging results.

The next period saw the expansion of the Benin empire. Oba Orhogbua was ambitious, and perhaps the first oba to have graduated from one of the Portuguese colonial schools. It appears that, following his father's death, some of the subjects stopped paying their annual tributes. Oba Orhogbua personally conducted a tribute-payment-drive by establishing his headquarters on Lagos Island. Lagos Island became known as *Eko* or 'king's camp'. From this base Oba Orhogbua fought Yorubaland successfully. Eventually his son was installed Eleko of Eko with an army division stationed permanently there to guard against insurrection.

Benin City was visited for the first time by an Englishman during Oba Orhogbua's reign. In 1553 James Windham reached Benin City in the company of Francisco Pinteado as his interpreter. From 1578 to 1590 frequent visits were made to Benin by English explorers such as John Bird, John Newton and James Welsh.

From 1700 to 1800 six obas ruled Benin. They were Ewuakpe, Ozuere, Akenzua I, Eresoyen, Akengbuda and Obanosa. The important constitutional change of the period, and one which has been strictly adhered to till today, is that only the eldest son of the oba should be crowned oba. There were, no doubt, minor difficulties arising from this, but they were taken care of either by fighting or negotiation. Otherwise the history of Benin during the period is a record of domestic affairs. Externally, however, contact was sporadically maintained with Europe by European visitors to Benin. For example, in 1704 D. V. Nyendael visited Benin City. Captain J. F. Landolphe made three visits to Benin in 1769, 1778 and 1787, while in 1815 John King, R.N. travelled to Benin.

The administration of the Benin empire
The Benin empire was extensive, including some parts of Ishan, Ivbiosakon, Urhobo-Isoko, Yorubaland and Iboland. In the case of the latter, there is still a marked Benin influence on Agbor, Asaba, Onitsha and Oguta.

Benin government, like many before or after, underwent changes and developments, but by the arrival of the British in the late nineteenth century, the pattern of the constitution was almost settled. First in the hierarchy of Benin government was, of course, the oba. The oba was regarded, and he claimed it, as the incarnation of the people's soul. The word *Oba* is a common title given to Yoruba and Benin kings. As a result of his divinity all the people in his empire were subject to him, and all authority derived from him. Thus royal officials held office at his pleasure.

Administratively the kingdom was partitioned into provincial units with the oba's agents acting as overseers. They included the oba's first son (Edaike), the queen-mother (Iyoba) and holders of Eghaevo titles. The title-holders were graded, the first grade being the Uzama. This consisted of seven titled chiefs considered the traditionally highest order of chieftaincy. They lived outside the city wall, where to a lesser degree each Uzama organized a court similar to the oba's.

The oba's executive or state council comprised the Uzama and the town and palace chiefs. It was to this body that the oba put all matters affecting the empire. But what might be called the oba's cabinet was drawn from among the palace chiefs. These were six in number and enjoyed the confidence of the oba. Opposition to government was from the town chiefs represented by the Iyase. Traditionally, the oba overcame opposition by sending an opposition leader to war from which he was not expected to return.

Though loyal to Benin, many of the so-called states within the empire were independent and in themselves constituted threats to the Benin kingdom. To determine the loyalty of a state, chalk (which in some parts of Nigeria signified good news and therefore occasion for rejoicing) was sent to the chiefs of the states on the accession of a new oba. Refusal to accept the chalk signified non-recognition of the oba, an act regarded as rebellion. Benin declared war on the rebel state and, if conquered, the ruler was taken to Benin and executed publicly. Benin had a standing army. Ezomo was the title of the supreme commander while the Ologbose acted as his lieutenant. Three groups supplied the war chiefs or captains – the Uzama, Eghaevo and Ekaiwe. Under each warrior was a well trained and disciplined battalion ready to go into action on orders. Native doctors accompanied the armies of Benin to cast magic spells upon the enemy. Among the war implements were the sword (*umozo*), a spear (*ogan*) and bows and arrows.

The position of Benin as an African state
The various accounts by Europeans who visited Benin should help us to summarize the position of this important African kingdom. The following conclusions may be made:

1. When the Europeans first appeared in Benin towards the end of the fifteenth century they found Benin already a well-organized state enjoying considerable influence in the hinterland of the Bight of Benin. The kingdom had a hierarchy of chiefs with the king of Benin at the head.

2. Materially and culturally the kingdom was rich. The inhabitants were far from primitive; the chief town, Benin City, was large and well-ordered. Its artistic achievements, first in the form of wood- and ivory-carving, and then in brass-work, were of a high standard. It would be interesting to know the sources of the prosperity in which the Europeans found Benin. For all we can see, a simple subsistence economy could hardly support such prosperity and a high level of culture. It was most probably largely based on external trade. Benin may have benefited from trade with the north through Oyo. Benin probably fed the southern terminus of the great trans-Saharan trade.

3. Frequent reference was made in the European accounts to the good-

naturedness of the Bini and this should give no surprise. A well-ordered kingdom may be expected to produce good-natured people. Government was effective; but there is hardly any evidence of tyrannical rule in the European accounts from the fifteenth to the eighteenth centuries. At the end of the period covered by this book, Captain John Adams was able to put on record that 'the government (of Benin) although monarchical appeared . . . mild.'

4. Constant slaving wars were, however, beginning to sap the strength of the kingdom of Benin, for frequent wars tend to lead to instability. As early as the beginning of the eighteenth century the critical Dutch traveller and writer Bosman, on visiting Benin City, thought he already saw signs of decay. Even so Bosman could not help admiring the efficient organization he saw in Benin. He was impressed by the just laws and the general honesty in which trade was conducted. The decay of Benin belongs to the nineteenth century.

5. The kingdom of Benin stands out as one of the finest examples of purely African statecraft unaided by foreign influence.

Dahomey

The kingdom of Dahomey, founded about 1625, rose steadily to prominence in the reign of Akaba who began to reign about 1690. The two principal languages of Dahomey are Fon and Adja, the former being closely related to Ewe. As the early history of the tribal groups is fragmentary, we may start by considering the history of Dahomey from the rise of the kingdom. It may be pointed out that the history of Dahomey is important for the student of African history not only for the purely historical developments but also for the extremely efficient internal organization that evolved around the monarchy of Dahomey.

The following traditional account is given of the founding of the kingdom of Dahomey. The king of the Fon-speaking people of the country, by name Tacoodonou or Dako, made war on Da, king of the inland town of Abomey. The Fon chief took Abomey after a long siege and quickly put Da to death. In fulfilment of a vow Dako had made during the siege, he cut open the belly of his stricken foe and placed his body under the foundation of a palace that he built at Abomey. Dako called his new palace Dahomey, from *Da*, the victim, and *homey*, his belly; that is, a house built in Da's belly. The date of the founding of the new kingdom of Dahomey with its capital established at Abomey was about 1625. Dako set up firmly the Dahomeyan dynasty known as Aladahonu.

The setting up of a new dynasty at Abomey was only the beginning of a long process of state-founding before Dahomey became a power to reckon with on the West African coast. A number of factors contributed to the rapid consolidation of power and extension of territory upon which Dahomey embarked after 1625. First, the aggressive expansion westward by Oyo towards the end of the seventeenth century must have taught the kings of Dahomey that the survival of their country lay largely in the development of centralized government. Probably also mere admiration for the strength of Oyo may have supplied a strong incentive for the centralization of authority in Dahomey. Thirdly, extension of the authority of Dahomey southward to the coast was a plain question of practical economics. Abomey was an inland capital 70 miles away from the sea and Dahomey had no access to the coast. On the coast were the Europeans willing to buy slaves in return for valuable commodities like guns and gunpowder, cloths and drinks. In the south the two sister states of Allada (Ardra) and Whydah stood in the way of Dahomey's direct trade and dealings with the Europeans. For many years it was consideration of the above situation that dictated the policy of the kings of Dahomey.

Expansion of Dahomey's authority
Dako's immediate successors, Whegbadja I and Akaba, finished the consolidation of the conquest of the Abomey plateau while the ambition of reaching and controlling the coast was achieved by Agadja, who succeeded Akaba. In the early eighteenth century Allada had established close relations with the Europeans on the coast and had become prosperous. And so had the coastal kingdom of Whydah. Trade between the coast and the interior was controlled to her great profit and advantage by this state. To break through this monopoly the Dahomeyans were determined to capture Allada, as well as Savi, the capital of Whydah. Agadja set himself this task. In 1724 he was able to conquer Allada by means of a surprise attack by the Dahomeyan army. Agadja took with him back to Abomey as prisoner an Englishman by name Bullfinch Lambe who happened to be in Allada when the town fell to the Dahomeyans. Lambe, who was released after two years in Abomey, has left an account which throws light on the wealth of the king of Dahomey even at the beginning of the eighteenth century. Lambe recorded that the king of Dahomey 'abounded in plate, wrought gold, and other sumptuous articles; that he had five and twenty pieces of cannon some of which weighed upwards of a thousand weight, which he took great delight in firing twice

every market day; that he was very liberal, but ... vain and proud, and considered having white men about him as a great addition to his grandeur'.

The conquest of Allada by Agadja placed Dahomey in direct contact with the kingdom of Whydah. Agadja's first move in a direct assault on the coast was to subdue Jaquin just east of Igelefe, the port of Whydah. After this he retired to his capital, Abomey. Early in 1727 Agadja returned to the attack on the south and captured Savi, the capital of the kingdom of Whydah. Agadja then moved against Whydah as a whole and took Igelefe, the port. This victory gave Dahomey complete access to the sea, and the Dahomeyans could now conduct unrestrained trade with the Europeans. However, the troubles of the king of Dahomey were not entirely over, for the inhabitants of the town of Whydah, who had fled to the lagoon near Little Popo, began to intrigue with the Europeans against Dahomey. Agadja had to send an expedition farther west. It may be recalled that during this period Dahomey was threatened with a series of invasions by armies from Oyo, and Agadja's efforts to establish Dahomeyan authority over the coast were weakened by being constantly harassed by Oyo. It must be pointed out that the strength of Oyo's control over Dahomey at this time was quite enormous: Oyo maintained a resident at Abomey and actively asserted suzerainty.

Tegbesu, who succeeded Agadja, also had to face invasions of Dahomey territory by armies from Oyo. In 1730 Abomey, the capital, was captured by Oyo and the king of Dahomey had to submit to humiliating terms of a tribute. The harassing of Dahomey by Oyo continued and the annual tribute was paid for eighty years. Under King Adahoozoo (also called Kpengla), 1774–89, the Dahomeyans were allowed to pay only half of the tribute because they had assisted Oyo in a siege of Badagry. It is interesting to note that in spite of all these troubles Adahoozoo found time to attend to trade with the Europeans. In 1779 he caused the road from Whydah to Abomey to be widened by his chiefs in order to facilitate the transport of slaves.

Agoglo succeeded Adahoozoo as king of Dahomey in 1789, but little is known about his reign. With the accession of Gezo in 1818 the fortunes of the Aladahonu dynasty of Dahomey rose quickly. In 1827 Gezo freed Dahomey from the hated tribute paid to Oyo, and began to extend the authority of Dahomey over the tribes to the west. The kingdoms of Dahomey and Asante developed friendship and mutual respect for each other's strength. It is said that Gezo was in direct contact with the king of Asante with whom he maintained diplomatic relations. Kumasi Palace in Abomey is a reminder of some sort of relation that must have existed between the two powerful kingdoms.

After gaining control of the south and of the coastal trade, especially in slaves, Dahomey began to expand to the north. The constant wars of expansion are explained by the fact that the surest way of feeding the slave markets on the coast was by making successful wars and raids. Gezo carried Dahomeyan arms far afield to the north and east. He ravaged Yoruba settlements west of Abeokuta. The successful expeditions by Dahomey against the Yoruba settlements were now possible because of the serious decline of the power of Oyo. But with the reign of Gezo we have already advanced far into the nineteenth century, which is outside our scope here. We may sum up the rise of Dahomey thus:

1. Until the seventeenth century Dahomey consisted only of small inland states with little strength.
2. In the seventeenth century Dako (or Tacoodonou, to give him his full name) of the Aladahonu dynasty set up what was really the beginning of modern Dahomey at Abomey.
3. Dahomey, which was an inland kingdom, wanted to ensure a monopoly of the trade with the Europeans. This desire led to Dahomey's attacks on the states of Allada and Whydah in particular.
4. The efforts of Dahomey to establish its authority and to extend its territory were seriously disturbed in the first half of the eighteenth century when Dahomey suffered many defeats and setbacks at the hands of Oyo armies. Dahomey had to pay tribute to Oyo and for nearly a century Dahomey seems to have stood in fear of Oyo.
5. In the early nineteenth century, under Gezo, Dahomey fully established its domination far afield and succeeded in building an empire. It was finally able to turn the tables against Oyo now disintegrating and becoming weak.
6. It should be remembered that the desire by the kingdom of Dahomey to control the slave trade on the Slave Coast, as she eventually did, was the main drive behind the steady growth of the kingdom.

Internal organization

The rise of Dahomey cannot be fully appreciated without some insight into the political and internal organization of the kingdom. The central fact about Dahomey is that the state was built around the person of the king who was regarded as being semi-divine. Most state business was transacted in the royal palace at Abomey. All control was kept in the hands of the king for whom there was surprising loyalty. The only recorded depositions are of King Adazan in 1818, and the overthrow and murder of his predecessor in a palace revolution in 1797. It is interesting to note that although the country was frequently at war, no serious rebellions took place. Succession to the king's stool passed from father to son, but there was no hard and fast rule that the eldest son of the king should succeed him. The king could nominate his successor, but the elders could put his nominee aside.

Nearly every activity of the Dahomeyan state was strictly controlled. In theory all property belonged to the king although in practice private property was tolerated. War booty was primarily the king's. Dahomey was a military state and everything was done to bring about unity of the state. All freemen were eligible to join the army, which was made formidable by stern discipline. Children were employed in carrying the baggage of soldiers to war so that they might gain experience in warfare. The army even had a corps of redoubtable female soldiers. The first appearance of these Amazons was in the reign of Agadja (1708–28) but they may have existed earlier.

The two principal officers of state were the Minga, who was commander in chief of the army, prime minister and chief executioner; and the Meu, who was master of ceremonies, collector of taxes and guardian of the royal princes and princesses. Besides these two there was the Yovoga, governor of the port of Whydah, who also controlled the movement of all Europeans in the country. Although the king of Dahomey welcomed the friendship and trade of the Europeans, he was always suspicious of the intentions of the White Men. If the European traders wanted to build new forts, they had the king's permission only to build a few miles inland and of mud and wood, and not right on the sea-shore and of stone and mortar as was the case in the nearby Gold Coast. The implication of such a precaution is clear: wood and mud forts built a few miles inland could not be effective in holding up any attack by Dahomeyan soldiers when such attack should become necessary. It should be clearly understood that the desire of the kings of Dahomey to watch the movement of Europeans and their activities in the country was not meant to put a restraint on trade with the Europeans. The kings of Dahomey were wise enough to encourage this trade in their own interests, for they could hardly have become as rich as they did if they really denied trade with the White Men. They used all means possible to increase the trade with the Europeans; but what they tried to ensure was that they, as kings and custodians of the well-being of Dahomey, were not tricked by any European.

The Minga and the Meu together acted as judges in the highest court of the country. The Yovoga also acted as head of the secret police. One principle of the Dahomeyan political system was to trust nobody. Spies were sent even after ministers and officers of state.

The management of the provinces of the kingdom was in the hands of deputies, probably six In all – one each for Abomey, Allada, Zaganada, Atakpame, Adja and Savalu. All these deputies had a series of subordinate chiefs. All the offices were hereditary but candidates had to receive confirmation from the king. The king as a rule did not permit a member of the royal family to hold any important post. Native chiefs of the conquered territories were allowed to retain their position if they showed disposition to obey, but Dahomeyan officers were always present to supervise. There was an efficient information system in the kingdom: reports were sent regularly to the king from the provinces. If a provincial chief lived near the capital, he went there once a month to report on his province to the king; if he lived far away, he travelled to make his report once every three months.

Every village had a chief in charge of the administration of justice. There was throughout Dahomey a deep respect for law. A king of the seventeenth century, Hwegbadja, reputed as a law-maker, is said to have punished his own son by the death sentence for breaking a law of the state.

There was a regular census of the population of Dahomey. Officers went round from time to time and kept the final figures of the census by depositing in the royal palace bags containing pebbles corresponding to the total number of people in the state. Officials stationed at Dahomeyan markets received tolls in cowrie shells. Heavy duty was levied on exports; slaves, cattle, goats and other commodities were taxed. Customs officials visited villages to assess and count taxable granaries during the harvest season.

The employment of women of remarkable memory in the king's palace was the answer to the running of the government machinery without the knowledge of writing. The king was always accompanied by a number of his official wives known as *Kposi* whose duty it was to memorize things said at interviews given by the king. The Kposi thus served both as stenographers and files. Each minister of state similarly had a female attendant in the palace who memorized and kept a record of things going on in that ministry.

Agriculture and trade were the most important economic activities of Dahomey. A money economy was encouraged and a leisured class grew up who employed artisans and capitalized the economic development of Dahomey. The most notable crafts were wood sculpture, brass-work, fashioning jewellery and making patterns on cloth.

The internal organization of the kingdom of Dahomey is admirable by any standards and shows the efficiency with which the African states of old conducted the business of government and statecraft.

9 States of the forest belt: Bono, Akwamu, Asante

Origins

The Asante, Fante, Akim, Akwapim, Kwahu and the Akwamu are the principal Akan or Twi-speaking peoples of modern Ghana. The Akan occupy the greater part of the forest zone to the west of the River Volta. They have a common tradition that their ancestors came from somewhere in the north, but it has not been possible to determine their original home in the northern grassland outside modern Ghana. It has been suggested that the ancestors of the Akan were among the fugitives who fled from the medieval kingdom of Ghana in the Western Sudan to avoid accepting the Islamic faith when the Almoravids invaded the kingdom during the second half of the eleventh century. This suggestion is, however, open to question. The extent of the flight from medieval Ghana as a result of the Almoravid invasion of A.D. 1076 cannot be fully assessed. It is, moreover, known that the fugitives from medieval Ghana organized themselves just outside the southern boundaries of the empire. In the absence of written records or archaeological evidence our main source of information on these questions is tradition; but there is no known Akan tradition that refers positively to an exodus from medieval Ghana. Tradition simply refers to the ancestors of the Akan as entering modern Ghana from the north.

In connection with the suggestion that the ancestors of the Akan came from medieval Ghana, attempts have been made to draw attention to the similarity of cultural practice in the medieval kingdom of the Western Sudan and among the Akan of today. For example, reference has been made to the incidence of matrilineal inheritance among the inhabitants of medieval Ghana and the Akan. It is not safe to jump to conclusions from the apparent similarity of custom. There are common traits of custom among the peoples of Western Africa in general. Moreover, it is far from certain whether matrilineal inheritance was the rule in medieval Ghana. The reason for the assumption is almost solely based upon a single statement in the account of medieval Ghana by the Arabic scholar El Bekri, namely, that the only persons allowed to wear tailored clothes in the medieval kingdom were the king and his heir presumptive, 'that is to say, his sister's son'. Even if inheritance on the mother's side was general in medieval Ghana, it would still not be safe to draw the conclusion that the matrilineal Akan came from the old Sudanese kingdom. Matrilineal inheritance is known to be practised among very widely separated peoples on the African continent who have no known relation with medieval Ghana. For example, some Bantu tribes in southern Africa follow matrilineal inheritance, as do the Hamitic Beja who live in the Horn of Africa near the Red Sea coast. It seems that for the present, and until we are able to learn more about the origins of the Akan, we have to be content with the bare traditional account that their ancestors entered modern Ghana from somewhere in the grass country of the north.

The Akan definitely remember that their ancestors, after wandering from the north between the Black Volta and the Comoe Rivers, ultimately settled in the region of modern Takyiman, Banda and Gyaman. From this region a group of them moved south into the forest and settled at the confluence of the Pra and Offin Rivers where, it has been suggested, they developed the distinctively Akan institutions and culture. It appears that the Akan ancestors entered Ghana in small groups and that they found a country sparsely but definitely inhabited already. The peoples collectively known as the Guans were already in possession of the country into which the Akan moved from the north. The Guan are today represented by the Anum, Kyerepong, Asebu, Afutu, Etsii and Breku peoples. The development of fusion following intermarriage of newcomers and existing people, to which constant reference has been made elsewhere, seems applicable to the Akan and the aborigines of the lands they entered in the region of modern Ghana. It seems likely also that the emergence of the Akan states in the forest country occurred many years after the arrival of the Akan ancestors from the north. The twelfth or thirteenth century appears to be a reasonable guess as the period when the ancestors of the Akan entered modern Ghana. The Akan states of the forest began to form about the beginning of the sixteenth century or during the second half of the previous century.

Bono

Bono is the earliest Akan state, having been founded about A.D. 1295.

It was established on the fringes of the forest and like other Akan states it developed a system of semi-military government.

The Bono kingdom was founded by immigrants from the north and it lasted for about five hundred years (c. 1295–1740). Its capital was Bono-Mansu, about one hundred miles north of the present site of Kumasi. Bono-Mansu is said to have been built by the first great ruler of Bono, Nana Asaman (c. 1295–1328). Bono tradition relates that the ancestors of the Bono people migrated from the Niger bend and settled for a time in the land of the Mossi. They were forced to move southward from the Mossi country because of the coming of the present ruling aristocracy of Mossi from Hausaland. Led by Nana Asaman, they crossed the Volta and settled some thirty miles east of present-day Takyiman at a place called Amowi. They left Amowi for another place called Yefri and finally moved to Bono-Mansu because of an earthquake which destroyed the caves in which they were living.

The Bono state was a great centre of civilization where many of the modern features of Akan chieftaincy seem to have been developed. The basis of this civilization was Bono's great wealth, mainly in the form of gold. It is interesting to note that the Takyiman state still possesses a very large quantity of articles made of gold. Bono enjoyed a prosperous trade with Mali and Songhai in the north. Gold is said to have been discovered in Bono during the reign of the second ruler of the kingdom, Nana Ameyaw I (c. 1328–63). The wealth was advertised in the markets of Mali and Songhai first by a prince of the royal house, and later by Nana Obunumankoma who, it is believed, introduced gold dust as a currency as well as gold weights for weighing the dust. He is also credited with establishing the *Sanaa* or treasury. Nana Obunumankoma also encouraged gold-smithing and golden jewellery for the royal house. Silver jewellery was also made for the queen-mother and her attendants. Gold was not only used for ornamental purposes, but also for household utensils – cups, bowls, basins and jugs. Golden lamps and lamp stands were made for use in the royal palace. The Asante were later to copy these developments from Bono.

Asante was in several ways influenced by Bono. Tradition records that when Opoku Ware of Asante defeated the Bono state in about 1720–25 many members of the Bono royal house were taken to Kumasi, among whom were the heir to the Bono stool and the queen-mother. On their arrival they were not at all impressed by what they saw in Kumasi in general and the royal court in particular. They therefore, it is said, taught the Asante rulers how to rule in great pomp and how to organize the court. Smiths and other craftsmen from Bono were brought over from Bono to teach Asante craftsmen most of the features of popular Asante crafts today. The Bono state was, however, in the end reduced to a satellite of the great Asante kingdom. The capital Bono-Mansu was destroyed and was replaced by Takyiman as the chief town of the area.

Akwamu

Early history

Akwamu is today a relatively small state extending over a small area around its capital of Akwamufie, east of the Volta Dam in the Republic of Ghana. However, some two to three hundred years ago Akwamu held hegemony over an astonishingly wide area in southern Ghana. It was in fact not only the first Akan state to build an impressive empire; it also developed an elaborate machinery of administration which became the model for a number of other Akan states, including Asante. Akwamu influences on the Akan peoples of Ghana as a whole appear to have been very considerable. The origins of the Akwamu state, like those of many other states of western Africa, are rather obscure. Our knowledge of events in Akwamu begins from about the middle of the seventeenth century, by which time Akwamu had already emerged as an imperial power on the coast. At its peak in 1710, the Akwamu empire covered a wide territory. It stretched along the coast from just east of Winneba to Whydah in Dahomey, and extended as far inland as Kwahu. It included the states of Agona, Akim, Obutu, Akwapim, Greater Accra, Krepi and Anlo. The old state of Ladoku, lying between Accra and the mouth of the Volta, also formed part of the Akwamu empire (Map 10, p. 121).

There was a tendency for the administrative centre of Akwamu to shift from place to place. During the early seventeenth century the state centred upon the neighbourhood of Asamankese and extended towards Anyinam. The present Akim Abuakwa towns of Akwatia and Kwabeng were within the Akwamu state. Many Akim towns have preserved traditions of former allegiance to Akwamu. Akwamu tradition points to Asamankese as the earliest capital of the state. From Asamankese the capital shifted to Nyanaoase near modern Nsawam and then to Nsaki near Aburi and at the foot of the western end of the Akwapim Range. In the end the capital moved yet again to its present site at Akwamufie across the Volta and locked in the hills of the Volta Gorge. It appears that before the imperial period Akwamu, which was then an inland state around the Upper Birim, was able to effect a kind of military union which embraced a number of associated tribes. It then managed to achieve wealth and power sufficient to enable it to embark upon an ambitious empire-building programme. There was a tendency to extend its power and influence eastward. After consolidating its position around the upper Birim and Densu Rivers, Akwamu gradually extended its control over the peoples occupying the Akwapim ridge from Aburi to Larteh. The latter town had come under Akwamu control and influence by 1646. It seems clear that by the middle of the seventeenth century nearly the whole of the modern state of Akwapim had fallen under Akwamu.

The main direction of the great expansion of Akwamu power was towards the east. This eastward expansion was dictated by practical considerations. North-west of Akwamu territory proper lay the powerful state of Akim for whose prestige and strength Akwamu seems to have developed respectful fear. To the south-west also were the strong Fante states against whom, as in the case of Akim, Akwamu had no desire to risk war. Thus the east was the one area safe for the expansion of Akwamu power. The Akwamu desire for eastward expansion was, however, greatly reinforced by economic considerations. Accra to the south-east had, by the middle of the seventeenth century, become the centre of operation for several European trading companies. The Portuguese, Dutch and English were all doing prosperous business in Accra. The trade in the Accra area was fed through paths leading to Accra from the interior. The control exercised by the Akwamu over these trade paths greatly irritated the Gas and led to constant friction between the two peoples. Eventually there occurred a big clash between Akwamu and Accra which led to the overthrow of Accra and its incorporation into the Akwamu empire.

The overthrow and annexation of Accra

After a long period of hesitation, the Akwamu king Ansa Sasraku launched a serious attack on Accra in 1677. Internal conflicts within the Ga state itself, largely the result of the tyrannical rule of the Ga Mantse (i.e. the king of the Accras), paved the way for an Akwamu victory in the struggle. Tradition has preserved the following account as the immediate cause of the war. An Akwamu prince had been sent to the court of the king of Accra for studies of some sort. The Accras circumcised the prince contrary to Akwamu royal custom, for no circumcised person could sit on the royal stool of Akwamu. The mutual acrimony that developed from the action of the Gas led finally to war with Akwamu. The Accra king at the time was Okai Koi.

The Akwamu made a determined attack on Ayawaso, the old capital of Accra. The Gas suffered a humiliating defeat: both Okai Koi and his eldest son and heir were captured and quickly put to death by the Akwamu. It appears that Okai Koi, whose régime had not been a popular one, was either let down or openly betrayed by some of his divisional chiefs. Ga tradition relates that Okai Koi cursed his treacherous subjects, prophesying that the Gas would always be plagued by treachery and disunity, and then he committed suicide.

After the fall of their inland capital of Ayawaso, the Gas continued to resist the Akwamu invaders. A younger son of Okai Koi moved the Ga capital to the present site of Accra, where he could count on the support and protection of European forts. Ansa Sasraku hesitated a little at first, but in 1680 and 1681 the Akwamu army was able to attack and overcome Small Accra on the coast, the town being burnt down. Many of the Gas fled along the coast to the east, some reaching as far as Little Popo and Whydah. For the next fifty years or so, Accra remained a province of Akwamu. When Akwamu power finally collapsed after 1730, the Gas were able to re-establish their independence, but politically things were not as they had been before the Akwamu conquest. 'The new Ga polity was to consist of small semi-autonomous stools, linked indeed by ties of kingship, culture and self-interest, but without the politically unifying force of a common sovereign ruler'.*

The extension of Akwamu power east of Accra

The country east of Accra, stretching from the town of Kpone up to Ada on the Volta, and extending inland to cover the modern Shai and Osudoku states, was during the seventeenth century the scene of a number of allied states collectively known as Ladoku. Along the coast of Ladoku were a number of trade posts set up by the Portuguese. It appears that between the fall of Great Accra (Ayawaso) in 1677 and that of Small Accra on the coast in 1680–81, the Akwamu had launched an invasion of Ladoku which was in the end annexed to Akwamu. Many of the people of Ladoku fled before the advancing Akwamu army. On the whole, however, the Akwamu adopted a moderate policy towards Ladoku. The king of Ladoku was at first allowed considerable autonomy in the internal affairs of his state. However, in 1688 the Akwamu became annoyed with the king of Ladoku for attempting to establish direct trade with the Europeans in Accra, and a fresh Akwamu attack on Ladoku

* Ivor Wilks, *Transactions of the Historical Society of Ghana*, Vol. III, Part 2, Achimota, 1957, p. 112.

began. Many people from Kpone and Prampram fled and settled in the country east of the Volta.

Ansa Sasraku, the king of Akwamu, died in 1689 not long after the second invasion of Ladoku. He left behind an impressive empire which was a real monument to his political and military skill. The Akwamu empire at the time of Ansa Sasraku's death stretched along the coast from Winneba to the Volta and embraced the important trade posts of the Europeans in and around Accra. It extended inland to cover the peoples occupying the Akwapim ridge. Akwamu had grown wealthy through tribute as well as the control of the trade of this vast area. A contemporary Dutch writer said: 'The king and his nobles . . . are so rich in gold and slaves that I am of the opinion this country possesses greater treasures than all those we have hitherto described taken together. The chief employments of the inhabitants are merchandise, agriculture and war; to which last they are particularly addicted'.*

Akwamu after Ansa Sasraku's death

Political developments in the Akwamu state appear somewhat confused after the death of Ansa Sasraku. Two men shared political power together in Akwamu as Ansa Sasraku's successors: an elderly person by name Basua shared the direction of affairs with a younger prince called Ado. The two men did not always agree on general policy. When Basua died in 1699, Ado was left in sole control of the state. In spite of the not infrequent friction between Basua and Ado, the Akwamu empire and Akwamu influence in general continued to grow apace. During the time of Basua, who was less favourably disposed than Ado towards the European traders on the coast, the Danish fort of Christiansborg at Osu fell under Akwamu control after one of the most interesting episodes in Afro-European relations on the Gold Coast.

In 1693 an Akwamu broker by name Asameni, who had managed to worm his way into the confidence of the Danes at Osu, one day turned up at Fort Christiansborg to arrange a deal. He told the Danes that he had brought some Akwamu people from up-country who wanted to purchase firearms. The Akwamu buyers were allowed inside the fort to inspect the guns for sale. Upon request they were given some powder with which to try the guns. But quickly the Akwamu people loaded the guns with shot they had brought in secretly tied in the folds of their cloths. They suddenly attacked the Danes, wounding several of the garrison. The Danish

* Ivor Wilks, *Transactions of the Historical Society of Ghana,* Vol. III, Part 2, Achimota, 1957, p. 119.

governor escaped by jumping through a window and the Akwamu seized the fort. They emptied the warehouse of its merchandise and Asameni took the gold he found locked up in a safe. The Akwamu king, Ado, in fact appointed Asameni governor of the fort and for a whole year he governed the fort in the name of his king. An Akwamu flag was hoisted on top of the fort and Asameni gave parties at the fort, received guests and visitors, and comported himself with all the dignity of a governor. After a year of occupation the Akwamu agreed to sell back the fort to the Danes.

The Akim launched a serious attack on Akwamu late in 1699 and Ado, who appears to have been taken unawares, had to negotiate for peace. Freed from the Akim threat, Ado was able in 1701 to resume the long-standing Akwamu campaigns in the east. The Akwamu army met with stiff resistance in the attempt to cross the Volta, but in the end it succeeded in doing so and carried its attack into Awuna country. Ado advanced on Little Popo, but his army had a very difficult task in overcoming the town. After taking Little Popo, Ado turned his men against Whydah, which soon fell to the Akwamu. Ado and his army were now some two hundred miles away from the Akwamu capital. Their victory over Whydah meant that Akwamu was in control of nearly two hundred and fifty miles of coastline from Agona in the west to Whydah in the east.

Ado had to hurry back home quickly with his army from Whydah in the middle of 1702 because of an alarming piece of news that had reached him. He heard that Denkyera had lately inflicted defeat on Asante. The news had spread great fear in Akwamu that Denkyera was about to form an alliance with Akim for an attack on Akwamu. By the middle of July 1702 Ado had managed to return to his capital with his army. The much-feared Akim-Denkyera attack on Akwamu, however, did not materialize. Ado died shortly after his return from Whydah and was succeeded by his brother Akwono.

Akwono proved to be a great king of the calibre of Ansa Sasraku. Like his predecessors he was determined to expand the Akwamu empire. But while his predecessors had directed their attention to the east Akwono decided to move northward, for he regarded it as unwise to try to push farther eastward beyond Whydah. In 1707 Akwono led an army across the Volta and attacked the Ewe of Peki, whom he overran. He pushed farther north and soon the Ho and Kpandu districts were under Akwamu control. After these quick victories, Akwono marched his army to the north-west and after recrossing the Volta began an invasion of Kwahu. Things did not go well for Akwono this time, and in

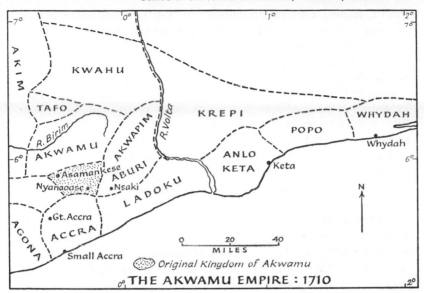

Map 10

1708 he had to give up the invasion and to take his army back to his capital. The Kwahu thus remained unsubdued. However, Akwono was not the man to admit defeat completely, and no sooner had he arrived back in his capital than he began to prepare a fresh expedition against Kwahu. In July 1708 he was back to the attack on Kwahu. The Kwahu were on this occasion soundly beaten and in July 1710 Ado made a triumphal return to his capital, having annexed Kwahu.

The year 1710 saw the Akwamu empire at its peak. It stretched 250 miles along the coast, from Agona to Whydah. It spread inland, covering nearly the whole of the modern Eastern Region of Ghana and the southern section of the Volta Region as well. But the wide Akwamu empire had inherent weaknesses. Firstly the enormous size of the empire was a serious drain on the administrative resources of Akwamu. As the empire expanded farther and farther to the east it grew out of easy reach and control from its capital lying in the west. Secondly Akim was on the lookout for a propitious moment to jump on its rival and put an end to its predominance.

The fall of the Akwamu empire

From the very beginning of the eighteenth century Akwamu began to live under the shadow of an Akim threat. The Akim, who had all the time been spreading southward from their original territory, began to cast envious eyes on some of the lands the Akwamu had taken into their empire. Furthermore, the Akim were anxious for their own benefit to break the Akwamu monopoly of the trade with the Europeans on the east coast. The prospects of a successful challenge by Akim of Akwamu hegemony improved as Akwamu's difficulties increased with the rapid expansion of her empire. By their treatment of subject peoples in their empire, the Akwamu were unconsciously paving the way for their over-throw by the Akim. For the Akwamu were not only tyrannical rulers of their empire: they were bad neighbours who made themselves a nuisance to the states near and around them. The sons of the Akwamu king behaved in an insulting manner in their dealings with the Akwamu chiefs. In many ways by 1730 the Akwamu empire was ready for rebellion.

In 1730 the king of Akim Kotuku, by name Frimpong Manso, rallied behind him a number of the disgruntled subject states of Akwamu. With such allies Frimpong Manso was able to harass and overrun the western parts of the Akwamu empire and finally reach the original Akwamu country. Each victory at the expense of the Akwamu won the Akim more allies from the oppressed areas of the Akwamu empire. The Akwamu were eventually forced to flee eastward until they found themselves pressed to the bank of the Volta by an Akim army hot on their heels. It was by sheer luck that the Akwamu were able to cross the Volta at Senchi to safety to their present abode east of the river. The defeat of Akwamu was a signal for their former subjects to declare their indepen-dence. The whole of the forest country around the Upper Pra and Birim fell to the Akim. The Akwamu subjects on the Akwapim ridge placed themselves under the protection of Akim. The Gas and the other states in the Akwamu empire to the east regained their independence. The once impressive Akwamu empire quickly disintegrated within a short period after the Akim attack. However, the Akwamu had succeeded in making a great impact on those states that had remained under their hegemony. The political and military organization of the Akwamu state influenced the various states that had come under the Akwamu empire. The Ga-Adangme peoples appear to have borrowed from Akwamu to enrich their own chieftainships. Akan military songs that still feature in Ga-Adangme festivals and ceremonies most probably originate from the period of Akwamu domination. There always existed close contact and co-operation between Akwamu and Asante. When Osei Tutu was re-called from Akwamu country to Kumasi to succeed his late uncle Obiri Yeboa as Asantehene, Okomfo Anokye of Akwamu agreed to accompany his young friend to Asante and to help him in his new position. The two men were actually provided with a body of Akwamu troops by the Akwamuhene. The Akwamu troops, said to number as many as three hundred, were given their own quarters in Kumasi. The presence of a detachment of Akwamu troops in Kumasi appears to have influenced the military organization of Asante. It is interesting to note that up to this day the second in command in most divisions of the Asante army is known as the Akwamuhene.

Asante

The Asante form the largest section of the Akan or Twi-speaking peoples. It has already been observed that the Akan appear to have made their first permanent settlement in modern Ghana in the area occupied today by Takyiman, Bona and Gyaman just outside the rain forest. From this area groups of the Akan migrated farther south into the forest belt. One such group, including the ancestors of the Akwamu, Fante and Asante, first migrated in a south-easterly direction and then down the Pra and Offin Rivers. After settling for some time at the confluence of the two rivers they dispersed again. Some moved south-eastward to establish Akwamu and Akim; the Fante moved southward to the coast; and the ancestors of the Asante turned northward to establish a number of states that ultimately came together to form the great Asante nation.

Popular Asante tradition claims the Adansi country west of Lake Bosumtwi as the centre of dispersion of the Asante. An old settlement called Asantemanso is remembered as the main point of dispersion in the lake district. From Asantemanso the Asante migrated in clans and family groups to new settlements such as Bekwai, Kwaman, Tafo, Kaase, Amakom, Mampong, Nsuta and Ejisu. For some time the new settlements remained disunited and weak. Some of them were actually the subjects of first the Adansi and then the Denkyera, whose centre of authority lay around the town of Dunkwa. The various Asante settlements or states began to unite into a political force during the course of the seventeenth century under the leadership of the clan called Oyoko (Map 11).

It is to be noted that the various Asante states were all established within twenty to thirty miles radius of modern Kumasi. This area has been referred to as the Kwaman Forest. An important trade route from Jenne and Timbuktu in the Western Sudan entered this area which was well known for its gold and kola. The area was also connected by a second trade route with Hausaland to the north-east. The establishment of the early Asante states in the Kwaman Forest was thus in all likelihood promoted by a desire to control trade with the Western Sudan. The importance in Asante history of this trade with the Western Sudan – the northern factor in Asante history – cannot be overemphasized.

It has already been pointed out that the early Asante states were subjected for a considerable time to domination by Denkyera. The

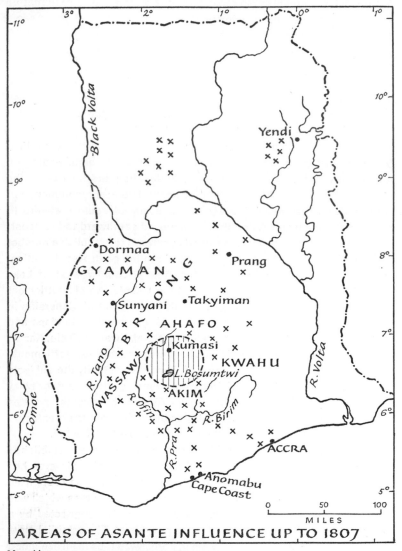

AREAS OF ASANTE INFLUENCE UP TO 1807

Map 11

Denkyera, like the Akwamu, were notorious for their tyrannical rule and there is little doubt that the burden of Denkyera rule was a factor in the union of the various Asante states into the great political and military power that Asante ultimately became. The acquisition of firearms by Asante from the Europeans on the coast, who sought and encouraged trade with Asante, played a large part in the mobilization of Asante forces which not only made possible the overthrow of the Denkyera yoke, but also paved the way for the great Asante empire of the eighteenth century.

Osei Tutu and the Asante Union

Osei Tutu's reign, which began in the later decades of the seventeenth century, is remembered in Asante royal history as the fourth. The first reign may be reckoned to have begun in the early decades of the seventeenth century. It was of two men, Twum and Antwi, who appear to have occupied the stool jointly. The second reign was that of Kobina Amanfi, and the third was of Oti Akenten. Oti Akenten is said to have set up his capital at Kwaman, from where he began to direct attacks against the Dormaa people living in the country to the north-west. Asante and Dormaa traditions have preserved different accounts of the issues in the struggle between the two Akan tribes (the Dormaa are also Akan). It is clear, however, that the struggle, like the oppression of Denkyera domination, necessitated some form of union among the various Asante states.

Oti Akenten probably died about 1660, and was succeeded by his nephew, Obiri Yeboa. Obiri Yeboa took up seriously the policy of conquest and expansion left by his uncle. Under Obiri Yeboa it can be said that the Asante union received its first great impetus. His main task was the attempt to unite the closely related Asante city-states in and around what is now the Kumasi municipality. Kwaman became a lively political centre. Obiri Yeboa met his death while fighting against the Dormaa and was succeeded by his nephew, Osei Tutu, popularly acclaimed by the Asante as the founder of the Asante union.

As a youth, Osei Tutu had been sent by his uncle, Obiri Yeboa, to the court of Boa Amponsem the Denkyerahene, but later he had to flee from Denkyera. He took refuge in the Akwamu country and it was there that he formed the memorable and lifelong friendship with the priest Kwame Frimpong Anokye, popularly known as Okomfo Anokye. It is generally believed that Okomfo Anokye was a native of Awukugua in Akwapim, where evidence of his magical feat is still said to exist. However, Anokye is also claimed today as an Asante.

When he returned to Asante to succeed his late uncle, Osei Tutu was

accompanied by Okomfo Anokye, and under the inspiration and leadership of the two men the Asante Union was finally completed in a way
that stood the test of time. Anokye has remained a legendary figure
among the Asante, and many are the wonderful magical feats attributed
to him. He was a very talented statesman who would have achieved
greatness whatever the circumstances. His greatest and best remembered achievement is bringing into being the Golden Stool of Asante.

Plenty of work awaited Osei Tutu and Okomfo Anokye. Osei Tutu
became king probably about 1680. He immediately took up his predecessor's work of uniting the Asante states and city-states around
Kumasi under the rule and leadership of the Oyoko clan. By a mixture of
diplomacy and magic, and with the invaluable advice and help of Okomfo
Anokye, Osei Tutu succeeded in welding the Asante states within twenty
or thirty miles radius of modern Kumasi into a solid union. He achieved
this step by step.

First the union was given a spiritual and lasting basis through the
Golden Stool. Okmofo Anokye is said to have brought down the Golden
Stool from the sky 'in a black cloud amidst rumblings'. The Asante have
always believed Okomfo Anokye's explanation that the stool embodies
the soul of the Asante Union.

Secondly Osei Tutu and his able minister, Anokye, established Kumasi
as the capital of the Asante Union. Osei Tutu was now not just Kumasihene: he was Asantehene, the king of the Asante.

Thirdly Osei Tutu, again with the help of Anokye, worked out a new
constitution for the Asante Union. At the head was the Kumasihene who
had now become the Asantehene. He ruled with the advice of Confederacy or Union Council consisting of the kings of the states forming
the union such as Bekwai, Juaben, Kumawu, Mampong and Tafo.

Fourthly the two great nation-builders established the *Odwira* as a
national festival at which the kings of the various states were to assemble
in Kumasi to pay allegiance to the Asantehene, to honour the dead, and
to settle any differences and disputes among themselves.

Lastly Osei Tutu set up for the Asante nation a military organization
believed to have been copied from Akwamu. When he was leaving
Akwamu country to succeed his late uncle, Osei Tutu is said to have
been provided with an escort of a few hundred Akwamu troops who
were permanently quartered in Kumasi. The new military order consisted of the van (Adonten), the rear (Kyidom), the right wing (Nifa) and
the left wing (Benkum). Each Asante state of the union was assigned a
place in command of one of the wings.

Conquest and expansion

Having established the Asante Union and a full military organization to support it, Osei Tutu began to wage wars of revenge, liberation and expansion. His first war was against the Dormaa who had killed his uncle and predecessor Obiri Yeboa. The Dormaa were defeated and they fled from their country to found a new state named Gyaman (that is to say, the state of people who had left their own home behind).

The states of Amakom and Tafo (now parts of Kumasi), as well as Offinso (fifteen miles north of Kumasi), had refused to submit to Osei Tutu representing the Oyoko clan. Osei Tutu fought and compelled the three states to submit and accept the union.

Having settled his immediate problems, Osei Tutu now turned the might of the Asante Union against the real enemy of Asante – Denkyera. Boa Amponsem, under whom Osei Tutu had served in Denkyera, was now dead. The new Denkyerahene was a rash young man called Ntim Gyakari. Gyakari is said to have haughtily demanded increased tribute from Asante, an action which finally led to war between the two states. The Denkyera crossed into Asante territory but were routed at Feyiase about ten miles from Kumasi. Ntim Gyakari was surprised and made prisoner. An Asante army eventually carried the war into Denkyera country and utterly defeated the Denkyera in a battle fought near the Offin River. The Asante subsequently annexed all Denkyera territory on the left bank of the Offin, and Denkyera began to pay tribute to Asante.

The Asante-Denkyera war may be traced to two causes. First, there was the natural desire by the Asante under Osei Tutu to regain their independence and put an end to Denkyera domination. Such a desire must have been reinforced by the confidence arising from the newly-founded union of Asante under the inspiration of Osei Tutu and Okomfo Anokye. But there was a good economic reason for the war. Already the Asante were beginning to show interest in trade with the Europeans on the coast. Asante trade paths to the coast, especially those leading to Cape Coast and Elmina, lay through Denkyera territory. To gain access to the sea and to be able to trade freely with the Europeans, Asante had to get rid of Denkyera power and interference.

The Asante found themselves at war with Akim shortly after the defeat of Denkyera. The people of Akim Kotoku had helped Denkyera against Asante. An Asante army invaded the Akim country and after fierce and bloody battles Akim was defeated and made tributary to Asante. The defeat of Akim by Asante took place about 1702. Osei Tutu appears to have used the years following his victory in further consolidating the

Asante Union, strengthening the bonds between Kumasi, the new capital, and the various divisions. Akim naturally resented Asante domination and from time to time attempted to revolt. Osei Tutu was in fact killed while he was engaged in suppressing an Akim revolt. According to popular tradition, the great Osei Tutu was ambushed and killed by the Akim as he was being carried by his men across the Pra. His death may have occurred in 1712 or five years later, in 1717. The double dates require some comment. The Asante-Denkyera war of 1701 has already been shown to have arisen partly from the desire of Osei Tutu to destroy the Denkyera hold on the trade paths leading to the European forts and posts on the coast. The Asante victory over Denkyera did in fact result in increased Asante trade with the Europeans on the coast now that Asante traders could frequent the coast without undue hindrance. However, in March 1712 an interesting report was made by the English at Cape Coast to the effect that Asante traders had suddenly stopped coming to Cape Coast 'because of the death of their king'. In 1717 the death of another Asante king was again reported. A further report by a European factor at Accra that year referred in the first place to an Asante-Akim conflict and secondly to a final peace between the two countries in 1718. It is not easy to state the true facts. If Osei Tutu's death had occurred in 1712, then another Asante king, whose death is the one reported as having taken place in 1717, must have occupied the Golden Stool before Opoku Ware, who is claimed by tradition to have immediately succeeded Osei Tutu. It may well be that the report of 1712 referred to the death of an important divisional chief of Asante but not of the Asantehene himself. In that case Osei Tutu's death may be reckoned as having occurred in 1717. The written record referring to an Asante-Akim conflict in 1717 reinforces the circumstances in which popular tradition places Osei Tutu's death. It is hard to imagine that Asante tradition could mistake the circumstances of the death of a hero king such as Osei Tutu. The one important fact is that so successfully had Osei Tutu and Okomfo Anokye built up the Asante Union that not even the shock of the great king's sudden death could shake the union. Both men could have attained greatness anywhere and in any age.

Asante from 1720–1807

When Osei Tutu became king, Asante territory roughly measured 40 miles by 30 miles. At the time of his death the area of the territory of the Asante Union had trebled. Osei Tutu and Okomfo Anokye's fundamental scheme for Asante Union was relatively simple. The different Asante groups were encouraged to forget old hatreds and rivalries quickly and completely for the good of all. Newcomers to the Union, even when they had been subdued through war, were absorbed into the Union on equal terms with the old groups. Their chiefs were accepted as full members of the Great Council of Asante, the *Abrempon*. It is even said that new members of the Union were made to forget their own traditional history. The plan for complete absorption worked quite well under Osei Tutu and Okomfo Anokye because, by and large, they were dealing with kindred groups with common customs. It would tend to be less successful as the Asante empire expanded and as non-Asante groups were called upon to merge their individual interests with those of the Union.

Asante tradition mentions that Osei Tutu was succeeded by his grand-nephew Opoku Ware. Opoku Ware's reign began about 1720. A succession dispute resulting in some confusion preceeded Opoku Ware's accession. In 1718 it was reported by the Dutch on the coast that Asante 'was much at variance between itself and had already fought twice between itself'. Then in early 1722 a further report was made of the arrival at Elmina of a triumphal embassy from the young king of Asante. It may be inferred that possibly by 1720 or 1721 Opoku Ware had succceeded in establishing himself on the Asante Stool after the confusion that had begun in 1717 or 1718. Definitely by 1724 Opoku Ware was the accepted Asantehene, for a Dutch record of that year referred to him by name as king of Asante. Opoku Ware enjoyed a long reign of some thirty years.

Taking advantage of the recent confusion within the Asante nation, Sefwi, Denkyera and Akwapim decided to help Akim to destroy the common threat posed by the growing power of Asante. Opoku Ware, however, proved equal to the difficult situation which faced him. He was able to defeat the Akim in two sharp battles fought on Akim territory. While Opoku Ware was away fighting the Akim, the Sefwi invaded Asante territory, sacked Kumasi and put to death members of the Asante royal family including Opoku Ware's own mother. The Sefwi opened the royal graves and stole gold ornaments with which the dead had been buried. On hearing the news, Opoku Ware rushed back home and sent an army after the Sefwi who were retiring to their country after the incursion. Amankwa Tia, chief of Bantama, leading the Asante army caught up with the Sefwi before they could cross the River Tano back into their home territory. The Sefwi were soundly beaten by Amankwa Tia's men and the Sefwihene, Ebirim Moro, was killed. All Sefwi territory beyond the Tano River was declared annexed by Asante.

E

Opoku Ware began to extend Asante power and influence northward by the invasion and conquest of Takyiman in 1723–4. After a short lull in this northward thrust, he moved his army against Banda and Gyaman. The pretext for attacking the latter state was that the chief of Gyaman, Abo Kofi, had made for himself a golden stool after the model of the great stool of Asante and had refused to surrender it to Opuku Ware on request. Both Takyiman and Gyaman were subdued between 1726 and 1740. After the successful campaigns in the north, Opoku Ware hurried down with his army to the south where the Akims, after their overthrow of Akwamu in 1730, were becoming extremely powerful, to the alarm of the Asante. The Akims and their allies were defeated and parts of Akim and Kwahu (the area now known as Asante-Akim) were annexed to Asante. The victorious Asante army pushed on farther south and annexed Akwapim, Akwamu and Ga-Adangme. In 1744 a section of the Asante army entered Accra. It had been a most successful series of campaigns, but rather unexpectedly the Asante army sought no further conquests in the south and retired home. Opoku Ware's last military preoccupation was a new series of campaigns in the north, ending in his overlordship of Gonja and Dagomba, between 1744 and 1746. Somewhat neglectful in purely administrative affairs, Opoku Ware however proved himself a brilliant war-lord. By the end of his reign he had succeeded in extending the Asante empire to the widest limit it ever attained. An Arabic record which has proved most useful in determining the date of Opoku Ware's death is revealing in the author's rejoicing at the news of the great Asantehene's death: 'May God curse him (i.e. Opoku Ware) ... gloats the recorder ... may he take his soul and cast it into fire. He it was who troubled the people of Gonja; continually and at all times did he trouble them. He seized their possessions. Whatever he wished so he did, for he was all powerful in his rule'. There can hardly be a more agreeable and true mixture of hatred and admiration from hostile quarters of the powerful position held by Opoku Ware as king of Asante and ruler of the Asante empire. He had held his own against great odds and actually succeeded in bringing a wide territory under the control of Asante. He was succeeded by his uncle, Kwasi Obodum. Obodum was of a peace-loving nature and was far advanced in years when he succeeded to the Asante Stool. The Akim rose against Asante, thinking the circumstances were opportune, but suffered defeat from the hands of the old Obodum.

After Kwasi Obodum's death in 1764, Osei Kodjo became Asantehene. He gave a good account of himself, continuing the policy of war and extension of the dominions of Asante. His first engagement was a war against an alliance of Gyaman, Wassaw, Denkyera and Kong, the last state lying far to the north. The alliance was called into being as the result of a threat by Osei Kodjo to punish the people of Banda who were alleged to have killed some Asante traders in their country. The Asante armies sent against the alliance suffered initial reverses, but managed in the end to win a convincing victory over the enemy. Banda and Wassaw were incorporated into the Asante empire; Denkyera and Gyaman were let off with an annual tribute to Asante.

Osei Kodjo had occasion to interfere in the affairs of the northern state of Dagomba outside the forest zone. One of two rivals claiming to be chief of Dagomba appealed to Asante for help. The other claimant is said to have sneered at the strength of Asante. The allegation prompted Osei Kodjo to dispatch an Asante army against Dagomba. The warriors of Dagomba, carrying spears and bows and arrows, were no match for the gun-bearing Asante. An annual tribute of slaves and cattle was imposed upon Dagomba. By his victory over Dagomba, Osei Kodjo had carried Asante domination far into the north. However, he was soon faced with trouble from the southern states of Akim and Akwapim. These two states resisted the claim by the Asante that they were in one way or another subject to Asante. It became necessary for Osei Kodjo to lead an army against the Akim and the Akwapim, but he found himself up against a number of southern states as allies of his main enemy, Akim.

In 1765, during the course of his wars in the south, Osei Kodjo found himself engaged in the first open conflict with the Fante on the coast. For many years the Fante and the Asante had remained at peace though mutual respect for the strength of each other. The Asante-Fante conflict of 1765 is worthy of notice because it is often wrongly thought that the Asante and the Fante met face to face in battle for the first time in the early years of the nineteenth century. The main cause of the open conflict between Asante and Fante in the middle of the eighteenth century and later to be renewed at the beginning of the following century, was the desire on the part of Asante to have free access to trade with the Europeans on the coast. It has already been pointed out that from the beginning of the eighteenth century the Asante had been showing active interest in trade with the Europeans on the coast. They wanted in particular to buy firearms and ammunition from the Europeans in exchange for slaves and gold. As the Asante empire expanded, the desire for trade with the Europeans grew apace. The extension of Asante military activities meant a greater demand for firearms and gunpowder. Repeated successful expeditions yielded large numbers of captives to be sold as slaves. The Asante trade routes to the coast, both to the east and west, invariably lay through hostile countries. The Akwamu, Akim, Akwapim and Denkyera were all seen by the Asante as obstructionists to trade with the Europeans on the coast. The Fante in particular had set up themselves as middlemen in the trade between the Asante and the Europeans, and the Asante had reason to believe that, as middlemen, the Fante often did not deal fairly with them. In circumstances like these the Asante were naturally ready to seize on any pretext to reduce their dependence on the southern tribes in trading with the Europeans. For many years the European merchants on the coast were reluctant to be drawn into any conflicts between the coast peoples, except when they felt that their commercial interests were in danger. When the Asante decided to take action against the Fante in the nineteenth century, the Europeans had to take notice of developments and felt compelled to take action to protect their interests.

The European trading companies were accustomed to paying moneys to the chiefs on whose lands their forts and trade posts stood either as rent for lease or as 'drink' to promote relations conducive to trade. The amounts payable were set down in notes and were paid to the chiefs who presented the notes. These notes changed hands mainly as a result of the fortunes of war. The Asantehene came into possession of a number of notes in this way. The Asantehene began to claim payment from the European merchants in respect of several forts. The claim could sometimes lead to misunderstanding between the Asante and the Europeans. The circumstances of trade and politics therefore brought the Asante and the Europeans, and in particular the British, face to face in friction.

It is now necessary to return to Osei Kodjo's campaigns in the south and his confrontation with the Fante. The activities of the Wassaw people played a leading part in the development of bad relations between Asante and Fante. The Wassaw state lying north-west of Fante and on the western trade route from Kumasi to the Fante coast was often an obstruction to Asante traders travelling to the coast. The Asante did not hide their dislike for Wassaw for this reason. The chief of the Wassaw state, fearing an invasion by the Asante, moved out with a large body of his subjects to a new home farther south towards Fanteland. This movement brought the Wassaw people right behind the coastal commercial centres of Sekondi, Shama and Komenda and thus placed them in a position to control the western trade from Kumasi more closely than ever before. To add insult to injury the Wassaw entered into alliance with the Denkyera and the Twifo in the west and with Accra and Akwamu in the east, and thus began to obstruct both the eastern and western routes to the coast from Asante.

In 1765 the energetic Osei Kodjo decided to break down the virtual blockade of the Asante trade routes to the coast by the Wassaw and their allies. In June 1765 Osei Kodjo led an army against the Wassaw who quickly fled into Fante country. The Asante persuaded the Fante to become their ally against the Wassaw and the two great powers defeated the Akim who were acting in support of Wassaw. Osei Kodjo decided to remain with his army in the south until the trade routes should become open again and safe for Asante traders. He pitched his camp at Abora right within Fante territory and just a few miles from the coast. The Fante then became suspicious of what the Asante were intending to do. A series of provocative acts committed by the Fante against Asante soldiers thoroughly broke up the alliance between Asante and Fante. The Asante, failing to obtain redress for the Fante acts of provocation in spite of repeated protests, began to fight the Fante. The Dutch and British merchants were seized with panic. However, lack of food for his army and the fact that the Asante were in the midst of hostile people persuaded Osei Kodjo to retire to Asante with his forces. The remaining years of the eighteenth century were filled with fear and rumours of renewed Asante invasion of the coast. However, Osei Kodjo was unable to return to the coast before he died in 1781.

Concerning Osei Kodjo's campaigns in the south in 1765 as well as the renewed Asante invasion of 1807, one point must be made clear in fairness to the Asante. The Asante were not the bloodthirsty warriors that they are often quite wrongly imagined to have been. When they fought the Fante on the coast who were often backed by the British, they had to do so because all negotiations had failed. As for the British, they hardly understood the Asante, about whom they were often grossly misinformed.

Osei Kodjo did not spend all his time fighting; he devoted himself to valuable reforms in the administration of the Asante state. He abolished some of the hereditary posts in the Kumasi state and replaced them with appointive ones. For example, he made the post of linguist (*Akeyame*) appointive rather than hereditary, as in the past. This reform ensured that the linguist was appointed mainly for his eloquence and intelligence. Osei Kodjo also created a ministry responsible for finance. Another important innovation made by Osei Kodjo was the creation of the post of *adamfo* at the Asantehene's court in Kumasi. The adamfo (i.e. friend) was a man resident at the Kumasi court (often a responsible chief of the Kumasi state) who acted on behalf of chiefs of the outlying provinces of the Asante empire. In 1776 Osei Kodjo is said to have dispatched three of his courtiers as district commissioners to the quarters of the Dutch, English and Danish trading companies in Accra. Asante commissioners were similarly posted at Abora, Shama and a number of other Fante states. A notable writer of African history has referred to the reforms of Osei Kodjo as the 'Kwadwoan revolution in government'.

Osei Bonsu and the Asante invasion of the coast, 1807

Osei Kodjo's successor, Osei Kwamina, was a boy of about ten on his accession. A regency controlled the affairs of state until Osei Kwamina came of age and decided to assume the rein of government. However, the young king soon became unacceptable to his subjects and was subsequently deposed. Osei Kwamina was succeeded by his younger brother, Opoku Fofie, but Fofie died only a few weeks after coming to the stool. In 1800 Osei Asibe Kwamina, popularly known in history as Osei Bonsu, became Asantehene. Osei Bonsu's reign saw the re-opening of the conflict between Asante and Fante that had started under Osei Kodjo in 1765. The British became involved in this renewed conflict.

The general background of the conflict between Asante and Fante on the coast has already been outlined. The conflict which occurred in 1807 in the reign of Osei Bonsu may be summed up briefly thus. Firstly the Asante were desirous of securing free access to trade with the Europeans on the coast. Secondly, the Fante were equally desirous of maintaining their lucrative position as middlemen in the trade between the Asante and the Europeans. Thirdly the British for their part were anxious to prevent Fanteland from falling under the political control of the Asante. The Asante became infuriated as the Fante from time to time between 1780 and 1800 attempted to close the trade paths from Kumasi converging on Cape Coast.

A relatively trifling affair touched off open hostilities between Asante and Fante in 1807. A sub-chief of Amo Adae's, the chief of Assin Api-menen, died and was buried according to custom with some gold ornaments on his body. After the funeral was over, a relative of Kwaku Aputae, chief of Assin Attandanso, is alleged to have returned to raid the grave. A dispute arose over the affair between Apimenen and Attan-danso, and Amo Adae in the end appealed to the Asantehene, and Adae and Kwaku Aputae as well as another chief of Attandanso, called Kwadwo Otibo, were summoned to Kumasi for settlement of the affair.

The Asantehene gave judgement in favour of Amo Adae, and Kwaku Aputae was ordered to pay compensation to the chief of Apimenem. Amo Adae later invaded Assin Attandanso as Aputae was slow in paying the compensation. The Asantehene ordered the two Assin chiefs to stop fighting pending further peaceful settlement. Kwaku Aputae unwisely executed the Asante messengers sent to him, and in the end the Asantehene sent an army against Kwaku Aputae. Aputae persuaded the old Kwadwo Otibo to join him to fight the Asante army. Aputae and Otibo later fled to seek refuge in Fanteland. The Fante chiefs, who were then gathered in council at Abora, refused to give up the two Assin chiefs to the Asante as the Asantehene had requested. The Asante army was therefore ordered to enter Fanteland and the two states were driven into open war over a relatively trifling affair. After a decisive Asante victory over the Fante army, Osei Bonsu was willing to negotiate a peaceful settlement of the whole matter, but the Fante chiefs refused to talk peace. The Asante army subsequently renewed the attack and defeated the Fante army for the second time at Abora, only four miles from Cape Coast.

Meanwhile the two Assin runaway chiefs, Aputae and Otibo, had fled to Anomabu where they threw themselves under the protection of the British governor, Colonel Torrane. Torrane agreed to protect them although he was in a state of great perplexity. He knew very little about the Asante and imagined that they were mere aggressors. The Asante army moved steadily towards the British fort at Anomabu which was in fact guarded by only a small garrison. The inhabitants of Anomabu in a panic fled to the fort for shelter to avoid facing the Asante army. Harassed exceedingly by the Asante assault on the fort, Torrane decided in the end to save the situation by handing over Aputae and Otibo to the Asantehene. On being surrendered to the Asante, the poor old and blind Kwadwo Otibo was instantly tortured to death. Aputae managed to make good his escape. Osei Bonsu was surprised at the unchivalrous behaviour of Torrane and meaningfully remarked: 'From the hour Torrane delivered up Otibo, I took the English for my friends, because I saw their object was trade only, and they did not care for the people'. Torrane later handed over to the Asantehene one half of the people who had flocked to the fort for shelter. The other half who fell to his possession he quickly sold into slavery.

The Asante army remained on the coast until October 1807, when the men left for Asante because of an outbreak of smallpox among them. The Asante invasion of 1807 was very significant. Things were never the same again in Asante-Fante relations. Firstly the image of the Fante as a great military power was destroyed. Secondly Asante became established as a coast power. The Asantehene is said to have taken a few steps into the foaming breakers on the beach, boasting that he was *Bonsu*, the whale, and lord of the sea. Lastly the British began to dread what might happen to them and their business following the establishment of Asante power on the coast. The Asante invasion of 1807 in short altered the balance in favour of the Asante.

10 The Ibos and the states of the Niger delta

The Niger delta extends for nearly three hundred miles along the Gulf of Guinea from the Benin River on the west to the Cross River on the east, and stretches inland to a depth of about one hundred and twenty miles. This vast area is criss-crossed by the Rivers Benin, Brass, Bonny, Kwa-Ibo, Cross and their tributaries as well as by numerous streams,

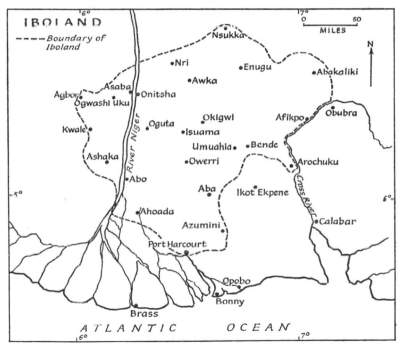

Map 12

E*

creeks and lagoons. The facilities for water transport in the delta are exceptional. 'There are hardly any roads existing in the Delta; the most trivial distance that a native requires to go, he generally achieves it in a canoe,' observed a nineteenth century visitor. Dr. Kenneth Dike has also pointed out that 'a canoe could be taken from Badagry (near Lagos) in the west of Nigeria to Rio de Rey in the east without going into the open sea'. In this well-watered area live some of the most robust and resource-ful peoples of the forest belt of West Africa. The tribal groups of people inhabiting the Niger delta include the Ibo, Ijaw, Jekiri, Ibibio (Efik) and the Calabari, to mention only the most important.

In one important aspect the history of the peoples of the Niger delta is different from that of the other forest states we have already dealt with. The peoples of the delta were, generally speaking, organized in small units rather than in the large complex states of the Yoruba, Asante and Dahomey. However, to say that the delta peoples were organized in rather small units is not to imply that they were living in isolation. There was even in early times considerable contact between the various peoples of the delta – contact created by war, trade and migration. The incidence of internal trade, especially trade with Europeans, led to the creation of strong city-states in the Niger delta, namely Brass, Bonny, New Calabar, Old Calabar, Warri and Opobo.

The Ibos

The populous Ibos live in the Eastern and part of the Western Provinces of Nigeria. They also inhabit some delta areas. That is to say, they politically occupy Onitsha, Owerri, three-quarters of Ogoja, parts of Warri and Benin Provinces.

The Ibo origin is still a matter of speculation. Researches are going on to locate it, but there are, as in the case of other tribes in Nigeria, many theories about it. Attempts that have been made to unravel the mystery of the origin through the word Ibo have not been successful.

The Ibos, according to Talbot, migrated from somewhere in the north between A.D. 1300 and 1400 and pushed towards the sea. Invading Arochuku and combining with the Ekoi, they drove away the Ibibio aborigines. In this process the invaders took possession of the Long Juju or Ebinopkabi oracle. The oracle of Long Juju was popularly believed by the peoples of the delta to possess omniscience as well as powers of bestowing fertility. In general the oracle was supposed to confer material gains of all sorts upon the consultant. The Ibo invaders used this oracle to boost their influence over the peoples of the area.

The Ibos themselves have no strong tradition of origin. They believe they have always lived within their geographical boundaries, and migrations were within and not from without. Jones and Mulhall, two notable writers, share this view. According to them 'The Ibo people have no tradition of migration from other parts of Africa and appear to have settled in the densely populated parts of Nri-Awka and Isuama areas for a long period and to have spread from there, their main expansion being southward, southeastward and eastward to the Cross River. They also crossed to Niger and spread into parts of the Benin and Warri provinces.'

Although the Ibos were segmented into clans, villages and compounds, they quickly came together, like the Hausa States in former times, to defend a common cause. For defence against external attack a standing army was always on hand comprising professional warriors drawn from Aba, Ohafia and Abriba and collectively known as the *Abams.*

That the Ibos rallied together in the face of a common enemy does not mean a centralized authority. The Ibos were not united under one paramount chief, and they lacked a central organ of government that might have served as a symbol of unity. However, there was political organization, in the sense that the needs of government were to some extent secured. To understand, therefore, Ibo political organization, one has to begin with the village which had a committee by which the community mind was expressed and public opinion crystalized.

Internal and external activities

Contact with non-Ibos seems to have been established quite early. Perhaps this was due to the fact that the country provided enough produce and raw materials by which the people lived and worked, and the surplus was made available to neighbouring tribes. For example, smithing was an important craft centred in the north-west at Awka and in the east (Cross River Ibos) at Abriba. The latter was the centre of smelted iron from the Abakaliki mines. The Abriba smiths therefore acted as distributors of smelted iron to other blacksmiths from the Item-Isuama area. The Awka blacksmiths obtained smelted iron from the people of Okpoho in Udi division where recently notes on the technique of iron-smelting were collected from the old men who remembered it from their childhood. The smiths supplied such utility articles as swords, javelins, spear-heads, axes, hoes, bolts, hinges, staples and a few ornaments like girdles, hair-combs, bracelets and anklets.

In addition to smithing, the Ibos were actively engaged in other forms of industry such as carving, pottery, carpentry, cloth-weaving (of which the Akwette cloth is a classic example) and salt manufacture. The latter was a very important industry, centred at Uburu and Abakaliki. The industry made the Uburu market 'the meeting point for many Ibo sub-tribes, the people coming from as far away as the Niger and its delta'.* There was, for example, a regular exchange of products with the Nupes and the Ijaws. As to trade relationship between the Ibos and the people of Northern Nigeria, Captain Beecroft† observed that the native tobacco he saw at Akunakuna (north-eastern Ibo) was prepared by the same method and smoked in long native pipes as he and his companions saw at Iddah in 1840. This observation suggested to him trade intercourse between the two peoples. Furthermore, a trade route passed through Iddah, Ogurugu and Nsukka to Nike to the north-east of Enugu, and by it the Hausa and Fulani traders brought to Iboland horses and firearms from the 'Dane-gun factories of the Anambara creeks on the east bank of the Niger.'‡ Trade in slaves was another factor that engendered intercourse with non-Ibos. Three principal slave routes in Ibo country have been recorded: firstly the Northern-Iddah and Ogurugu to Nike; secondly the Southern-Awka and Bende to Arochuku; and thirdly the Eastern Nkalagu, and to Cross River. All the slaves from the first and second sources were deposited at Nike, and from there to Uzuakoli slave market called Abagwu. From Abagwu they were taken to Bende and finally sold to the Aros who in turn sold them to Bonny and New Calabar middlemen. The slaves sold were not only Ibos but also people of Northern Nigerian origin.

Contact with Europeans

The slave trade was the major factor that brought the Ibos into contact with the Europeans. It is not certain whether any White Man reached Iboland before the nineteenth century. It has been suggested that the Portuguese probably reached Arochuku in the sixteenth century for trade in slaves. There is no doubt, however, that many Ibos had come into contact personally with Europeans either as slave dealers or slaves. Dr. Dapper, writing in 1688, said that the Ibos brought down to the Kalabari River slaves and foodstuffs such as bananas, palm oil, pigs, goats and chickens to sell to Europeans on board ship. Writing in about

* *Nigeria*, No. 56, 1958, pp. 87–96.
† Beecroft was an Englishman who explored the Benin and Old Calabar Rivers and travelled up the Niger to Lokoja between 1835 and 1842.
‡ W. R. G. Horton, 'The Ohu System of slavery in a northern Ibo village', pp. 11–12.

1699, Barbot referred to the Ibos whom he called 'Hackbous' as 'warlike, predatory and lustily tall'. He further stated that they had two markets every week for slaves and provisions. John Adams later (1790) described the Ibo slave market, which he said supplied 16,000 slaves annually.

The earliest recorded appearance of a White Man in an Ibo town was in 1830 when Richard and John Lander were taken prisoner at Asaba and transported to Aboh where they met 'the dreaded Obie, King of the Eboe country'.* The encounter with the Obi of Aboh led the Landers to describe the Ibos as 'the most inhospitable tribe, most covetous and uncivil, and having a savage appearance'. A successful attempt at founding a station for trading and evangelism was made at Onitsha in the mid-nineteenth century (1857) by William Baikle and Samuel Adjai Crowther.

Consequent upon the external contact some Ibos experienced cultural changes. For example, the Ibo slave dealers exchanged slaves for copper rods which were used for armlets and necklets. They were also supplied with European arms which by 1800 had become handy for both fighting and hunting. Adams's report about the volume of trade in slaves was in part responsible for the abolitionist agreements with native chiefs in the 1840s.

The Ibibios

In their study of *Ibo and Ibio-speaking Peoples of Nigeria*, Forde and Jones have subdivided the Ibibio tribe into six main groups – Eastern or Ibibio Proper, Western or Annang, Northern or Enyong, Southern or Eket, Delta or Andoni-Ibeno and Riverain or Efik. The people who make up these groups have no strong tradition of origin nor of the time of arrival in their present location. Contrary to a theory of origin from Ibom in Arochuku, tradition mentions the western bank of the Cross River called in Efik *Akwa Akpa* as the first place of abode of all the Ibibio people. There was a degree of movement from wherever the original settlement might have been, resulting in groups which have since grown into sub-tribes (Map 13).

One such sub-tribe are the Efiks. The word Efik derives from the Ibibio *fik* which was used to describe Offiong, the ruler of Afagha people or the early Ibibio settlers at the mouth of Calabar River. Offiong was said to have been tyrannical and oppresive. Thus in Ibibio *fik* means 'to op-

---

* Richard and John Lander, *Journal of an expedition to explore the course and termination of the Niger, Vol. 2*, Harper, New York, 1837, p. 213.

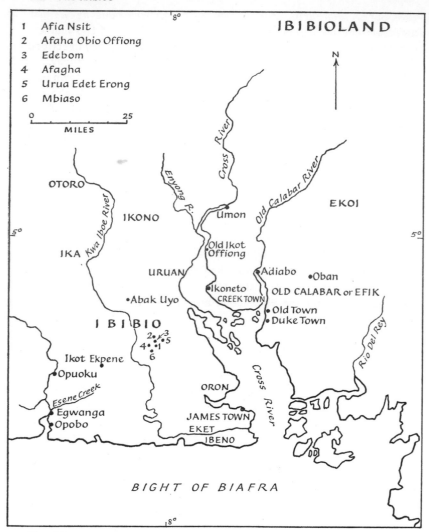

1   Afia Nsit
2   Afaha Obio Offiong
3   Edebom
4   Afagha
5   Urua Edet Erong
6   Mbiaso

IBIBIOLAND

Map 13

press' and so Offiong and his family were associated with the name Efik, meaning 'those who rule with iron hands.' It eventually became a term of reproach, even though his direct descendants were known by that name. It is further said that such direct descendants include Ibibios in present-day Calabar.

Eventually these inhabitants of Creek Town spread out to other smaller settlements, and together were known as Obio Efik or Efik Towns – the present Calabar. It is because Calabar became more civilized as a result of early European contact that the name Efik became a tribal name in place of Afagha or Ibibio.

Calabar

The name *Calabar* appeared first on Dutch maps of the seventeenth century, and first applied to the Cross River. Calabar may therefore be European in origin, deriving from *Kalbonger, Calabaros* or *Calapongas* used to describe the inhabitants of Rio del Rey. The name was in error given to the Cross River estuary and to distinguish it from the Kalabari River the words 'Old' and 'New' were employed. Thus the Cross River was known as the Old Calabar River, and the Calabar River named New Calabar River.

A quarrel which occurred among the settlers at Creek Town resulted in a further movement by some of the dissenters. Their settling at Obutong or Old Town agitated the minds of the leading Creek Town business men who would not tolerate trade competition from the new settlers at Obutong. To counteract the rivalry, the traders moved to Akwa-Akpa, which they renamed Duke or New Town.

Each of the Calabar Towns or colonies was organized with a view to trading and defence. A leader soon emerged representing the colonists before the European merchants. Thus there arose chiefs from each town. Eyo (Oyo) from Creek Town; Robin and William from Obutong; Duke Ephraim (Effium); and King John from Duke Town. Each town vied with the other and not infrequently one town would wage war against the other. For example, in about 1770 Akwa Akpa waylaid the chiefs of Obutong who had been invited for a conference on an English ship and killed many of them. By 1790 Duke Town had grown to be the commercial centre of the Calabar district and under Effum (Duke Ephraim) the White Men were respected and allowed freedom. After subduing Obutong, Duke Town concentrated upon Creek Town, whose King Honesty I fell by intrigue. He was succeeded by an unwise brother who reduced Creek Town to a second rate colony. Thus for practical purposes Duke Town became the most important of all the Calabar towns.

External contacts

Although the Portuguese, the earliest European traders in the Bight of Biafara, may not have used the Cross River, since their records are silent on it and the Efiks, by the seventeenth century the Dutch referred to the Efik settlements of the Cross River as Old Calabar. Calabar trade activities in the seventeenth century are attested by John Barbot. According to him brass rings, called by the natives *bochie*, were in great demand for the arms or legs. The rings were made by the natives from small bars of copper three feet long and weighing about a pound and a quarter. These were imported by the Dutch and the English. Not only were the bars used as rings, but also as currency. 'The blacks there (Old Calabar River)', John Barbot wrote, 'reckon by copper bars, reducing all sorts of goods to such bars; for example, one bar of iron, four copper bars; a man slave for thirty-eight, and a woman slave for thirty-seven or thirty-six copper bars.' John Adams also mentions Calabar as one of the recipients of Ibo slaves.

Apart from material benefits that accrued particularly to the kings and middlemen, a cultural change was visible among the Efiks. Notwithstanding the White Man's goods that were often exchanged for slaves, some Efiks adopted European names. Some of these were undoubtedly wrongly pronounced, but they soon stuck to their owners who were ever after known by them. Such names as Ephraim for Effiom, Cobham for Akabom, Achibong for Asibong, to name but a few, are examples.

Language difficulties were no doubt responsible for English translation of the names, and indeed hampered trade transactions, but the difficulty was overcome by learning to speak 'broken' or pidgin English. Both the white and the black traders had to learn to speak it, and in time this new language filtered through the delta commercial towns to hinterland tribes. It is of little wonder, therefore, that when in the nineteenth century the missionaries arrived, there were native interpreters on hand.

Administratively the government of the Calabar towns developed to meet trading demands. Although Creek Town, Duke Town and Obutong were republics, they had kings who, to all intents and purposes, were dictatorial. Perhaps a form of dictatorship was necessary to enforce trade regulations among the subjects. As for the rest of the tribe, government was by consultation and, as in Iboland, it began on the village level. Whether in the more advanced towns or Calabar or the rural areas of Efikland, government was rooted in religion and magic. In this connection reference must be made to the Ekpo Society or secret cult that combined political and religious functions. Indeed it was, until comparatively recently, the effective government of the Efiks, and served as a bond of unity among the Calabar trading units.

A remarkable feature of Ibibio history was the evolution of picture writing which had its counterpart among the Ibos and the Ekoi. The pictogram, like the earliest Egyptian writing, was inscribed on walls and body with sharp pointed instruments. It was also engraved on tombs to indicate perhaps how the man, particularly if he was a chief, died. Sometimes the writing was in the form of drawing. For example, if the deceased was a hunter, a picture of a bow and arrow was inscribed on the wall of his house. This drawing-form of writing was developed into what looked like a symbolic writing. Like the Ibo form of writing it was called Nsibidi script and was taught only to members of the Ekpo Society. The Nsbidi was discovered in Calabar in 1910, five years after the Ibo Nsibidi.

Nsibidi never developed beyond the pictogram stage. By the time it was discovered by the European both in Ibo and Efikland, the English alphabet was being taught.

The Ijos (Ijaws)

The people of Ijo inhabit the delta. Taken together, the origin of the Ijos is not clear-cut. The suggestion, however, is that migration was from the Binin-Abgor hinterland. The Ijo tribe today consists of four main sub-tribes – Brass, Kalabari, Bonny and Warri (Map 14).

Brass

According to tradition Brass was founded by three men named Obolo, Olodia and Onyo. The camps they established were each called after them – Oboloama, Olodiama and Onyoama. The origin of these people is not known, but it is said that they came from Benin as fishermen.

The three towns did not last long because of civil wars and the outbreak of smallpox epidemics. Remnants of the inhabitants moved away from the original towns and established new homes. The Onyoamas founded the towns of Segu, Sangana and Oboloama at Ekuleama (named after the headchief, Ekule). The people of Olodiama do not seem to have founded a new town either because they died out or chose to fuse with their neighbours.

A few years later a fresh body of immigrants arrived from Benin as fugitives and became the Iselemas. They were kindly received in Nembe by the king and given land for farming. Having stayed for a short time at Amasare-Polo, the farmland, they were moved to another spot called Oru-Ama-Biri, where they were free to worship the male god they had brought from Benin. The fugitives, it is said, were the progenitors of the present Brass people.

The original settlers, that is the people of Onyoama and Oboloama,

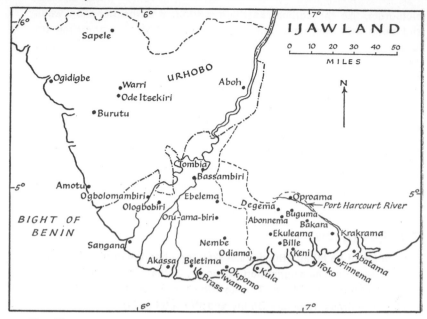

Map 14

with the later immigrants came to be included within the area known today as Brass. The name 'Brass' was given to the country by the Portuguese who traded in slaves from 1472 to 1600. The Brass people often expressed disapproval of a trade deal with the word 'Ba-Ra-Sin', meaning 'Hands off', 'Let go'. This earned them the name *Barasin*, which was eventually contracted to 'Brass' by the English merchants.

The Obimas migrated from Benin to Brass as fishermen and decided to settle there. The king would not accede to their request for inland settlement and as a result they lived at the mouth of Brass River from where they branched out into separate areas which became Opkomo or Big Fishtown, Iwama or Small Fishtown, Beletima, Akassa, Odiama, Ologbobiri and Ebelema.

In addition to the above settlements which later grew into self-contained towns, other towns of importance existed in Brass. Notable among them is Nembe, which grew into the capital of Brass and consists of two well-defined towns – the present Ogbolomabiri and Bassambiri.

The first known Brass chief was Ekule. After him ruled seven chiefs and the last in that line was Basua. Following Basua's death in about 1700, there arose a palace quarrel between his two sons Mingi I and

Ogbodo for the throne. The quarrel resulted in a civil fight between two factions, each supporting a candidate. Ogbolomabiri supported Mingi I and Bassambiri favoured Ogbodo. No one candidate emerged victorious, and consequently there evolved two lines of kingship. Mingi I became the first king of Bassambiri. By 1800 four kings – Mingi I, Mingi II, Ghore III and Forday IV had ruled over Ogbolomabiri, while Obodo, Gbolewi, Dede and Ramuna ruled over Bassambiri.

Kalabari

Kalabari, after whom the early community was named, is said to have been the founder of the Kalabari sub-tribe. He had a son named Ende or Ede, who led a migratory group from an Ibo village, Amafo, then situated on the western bank of New Calabar River. While here the settlers are said to have welcomed another migratory group from the Efik tribe whose leader was Opukoroye, and who introduced the Owame Akaso god to the new area. Together both groups became known as Kalabari, who eventually split into two groups – Endeme and Korome. Among the Endeme group was an Ibo doctor, Kamalu, who emerged as the leader. This same name appears in the history of Bonny.

At best the Kalabari people were a mixture of different sub-tribes who had peopled Ijo country. That is to say, the original Kalabarians were Ijos, but as a result of migrations there was a mixture of Ibo and Efik elements. Population growth led to expansion towards the Calabar and Imo River whose banks formed temporary settlements, but these settlements were eventually transferred southward to the Rio Real, where the Kalabari and Bonny people established themselves permanently.

The principal towns of Kalabari are Buguma, Abonnema, Bakara, Tombia, Krakrama, Ifoko, Keni (pronounced Ke), Kula, Dekeona (Degema), Sokin, Terima, Okpo, Oporoama, Sema, Sangama, Oru-Sangama, Angulama, Bukuma, Minama and Bille. Some of the towns were founded in the mid-nineteenth century, but others, such as Krakrama, Ifoko, Keni, Kula and Sangama, are ancient.

A similar migratory movement holds good for many of the towns of the Ijo group. For example the Krika, later corrupted to Okrika and meaning 'we are not different people', were among the small groups from central Ijo who settled near the present town of Port Harcourt where they acted as suppliers of fish to the principal towns of Kalabari.

Bonny

Bonny was founded by a great hunter called Alagbariya. This name suggests Ibo origin and means 'special type of land'. Since the site was particularly suitable for a port, it is likely that the name was not that of a particular individual but a descriptive word for the site. Similarly, the original name Okoloma means 'a town full of birds', suggesting an uninhabited plot of land. Who these inhabitants were is difficult to say, but they might have been Ibos. Another tradition ascribes the origin of Bonny to the Ndoki sub-tribe that today occupies the southern area of the Imo River. The Ndoki people are said to have been Ijos, but that they dispersed to the Rio Real area where two offshoots of the Ijos were already settled – Abalama and Iyankpo. A group of new arrivals drove away the Abalama people and for fear of a similar attack the Iyankpo dispersed. Those of them who moved became the people of Tombia in Kalabari while those who remained became the Finnema people of Bonny. The two traditions or origin have a common denominator, namely, Ibo connection. Undoubtedly there was a close commercial and cultural contact with the Ibo tribe. Early Bonny trade which attracted the Ibos was salt obtained from the evaporation of sea-water, the Ibos in return supplied foodstuffs which the riverain peoples lacked. In the early days of the slave trade Bonny depended upon the Ibos for most of its needs. It is said that one Asimini introduced the trade in slaves to Bonny by opening trade relations with an Ndoki chief whose daughter he married. The name of the Ndoki chief was Azuogu, and his grandson, Kamalu, later became the king of Bonny. It is further said that both Amachiri and Pepple, who became the kings of New Calabar and Bonny, were of Ibo descent.

Perhaps as a result of this contact the Ibo language was more widely spoken in Bonny than any other section of the Ijo tribe. That is one reason for assigning a common origin to both peoples.

Warri

There is a tantalizing hint that the Warri people were originally Ijos but that they came into prominence with the arrival, in about the fifteenth century, of Oginuwa (Ginuwa) from Benin. He was the ousted son of the Oba of Benin who out of desperation took refuge in the delta. It appears that he attracted many followers, notably slaves from Benin, some of whom settled at Ogidigbe, Amotu and Burutu. Eventually there was a concentration of settlers at Ode-Itsekiri which later became the capital town. These runaways were known in Benin as *Iwerri*. The town was therefore called Warri by the Portuguese in about the sixteenth century.

Farther north of the Forcados River live the Sobo (Urhobo) people whose forefathers were a section of migrants to Warri. As early as the fifteenth century the Sobo people were great traders in slaves, palm oil, leopard skins and blue beads (coris) and pepper. These articles of merchandise were sold to the Portuguese.

An offshoot of Urhobo was Okpe, which became known as Sapele. The name derived from Urhie-Apele which was later spelt Uriapele, meaning Julu River. *Urhie* is River and *Apele* the name of a juju.

The Olu (king) of Warri was Anthonio de Mingo, whose father, Mingi, had been to Portugal and there married a Portuguese girl, brought her home and by her had a son, Anthonio. On his return home Mingi requested Pope Innocent X to send missionaries to teach his people. A prefect and three priests from the Capuchin Mission were sent to Warri in 1682.

Until the eighteenth century, the Olu of Warri acknowledged the suzerainty of Benin. It is not surprising, therefore, that Warri culture is more related to Benin than Ijo. Moreover, the royal state sword, ivory trumpets, coral-beaded crowns and robes and chieftaincy titles were inherited from Benin. The king's palace was built in the Benin style but it was smaller and less imposing. In the exercise of authority and power he was quasi-independent. Three councillors assisted in the administration, and to each of them he assigned sections of the kingdom to rule in his name. In addition to the councillors the king appointed customs officers called Wacoa.

Trade activities in the delta area

The delta region was a great centre for the slave trade. We have earlier called attention in passing to the report on the West African slave trade made by Captain John Adams. Referring to Bonny and New and Old Calabar, he wrote:

'This place (Bonny) is the wholesale market for slaves, as not fewer than 20,000 are annually sold here; 16,000 of whom are natives of nation, called Heebo, so that this single nation has not exported a less number of its people during the last twenty years, than 320,000; and those of the same nation sold at New and Old Calabar, probably amounted in the same period of time to 50,000 more, making an aggregate amount of 370,000 Heebos.'*

As a result of the trade and subsequent contact with Europeans, the delta people imbibed European culture much earlier than the hinterland people, and developed into what Dr. Dike has described as 'city-states'.

* Captain John Adams, *Remarks on the country extending from Cape Palmas to River Congo*, London, 1823, p. 129.

States like Bonny, Kalabari and Warri were monarchial while Calabar and Brass were republican.'* Laws were made mainly to protect trade, and were enforced on the village level by the House Rule system. The House Rule system was a very important development in the delta states. The House was in fact an extended family group or local community under the leadership and rule of a family head. The head of the House quite often imposed a strict control over the members of the House. Some of the members of the House were sometimes reduced to a servile status. The head of the House, and those in whose interest the system grew, became in time capitalist overlords.

* K. O. Dike, *Trade and Politics in the Niger Delta*, Clarendon Press, Oxford, 1956, p. 31.

11 West Africa and the Europeans

Exploration and the development of trade

Ancient times

Some two thousand years before the Portuguese exploration of the fifteenth century A.D. brave sailors from the ancient world are said to have visited the coast of West Africa. There are accounts by the ancient Greek historian Herodotus that about the year 600 B.C. Phoenician sailors were commissioned by King Necho of Egypt to sail round the entire coastline of Africa to establish that the continent was a huge island joined only to Asia Minor by the narrow neck of land now cut through by the Suez Canal. The Phoenicians were among the most skilful sailors of the ancient world and their ships sailed over all the known seas of the time. Herodotus's account states that the Phoenicians took two full years to circumnavigate Africa. Starting from the Red Sea, they sailed round the southern tip of Africa, now known as the Cape of Good Hope, and then sailed northward, hugging the coast until they eventually entered the Mediterranean Sea and returned home to Egypt.

Some historians have expressed doubts about the feat by the Phoenician sailors. It has been pointed out that the difficulties of navigation involved in the 16,000 mile voyage would be too much for the sailing ships and the navigational skills at the disposal of the ancients. The rough seas and the adverse winds in particular of the West African coast, are thought to have been well-nigh insurmountable in ancient times. It is a great pity that the accounts by Herodotus should be lacking in facts and details that could establish beyond reasonable doubt the feat attributed to the Phoenicians.

Another expedition from North Africa down to the coast of West Africa is mentioned as having taken place in the sixth century B.C. A Carthaginian called Hano is reported to have sailed down the coast of West Africa beyond Morocco with 60 ships and 3,000 colonists. Again historians are not agreed as to how far Hano and his countrymen reached on the coast of West Africa. Some believe that the Carthaginians sailed as far as the Cameroon mountains, while others have suggested that they did not navigate farther than just beyond the southern Moroccan coast to Mt. Kakoulina near Conakry.

The Carthaginians, like their kinsmen the Phoenicians, were great sailors of the ancient world. It is interesting to note that the ancient people to whom the great navigational feats concerning Africa have been attributed should be the most likely people to be capable of the achievement. That the expeditions by the Phoenicians and the Carthaginians were attempted should be beyond doubt. What is not known for certain is what was actually achieved in each case.

Preparation and aims of the Portuguese explorations

Over five hundred years ago the Portuguese began memorable voyages to the coast of West Africa, later to be known as the Guinea Coast. The voyages were for some forty years organized by Prince Henry of Portugal, popularly known as 'the Navigator', although as a matter of fact he never himself sailed out on any of the voyages he directed. At the beginning of the fifteenth century Portugal was most suited to undertake great oversea voyages. The country had mobilized its natural resources considerably under the Avis dynasty which began in 1385 with the reign of King John I. At the beginning of the fifteenth century Portugal possessed an influential and favoured middle class with ships and capital for oversea trade, speculation and adventure. A fast sailing-ship, the caravel, was increasingly being put to sea. A very useful navigational instrument called the astrolabe, employed for measuring attitudes of stars, had become a great asset to long-distance navigation out of the sight of land. Very helpful nautical charts and maps of greater accuracy than before were also available. The Portuguese of Prince Henry's time were far better equipped for undertaking distant voyages than any other people in Europe. Henry was able to assemble at Sagres, where he established a school for navigation at his own expense, the most up-to-date devices of navigation. The best astronomers, geographers and map-makers in Europe flocked round Henry at Sagres.

Prince Henry had a number of aims in view in organizing the voyages of exploration to the coast of West Africa. Firstly he was seeking to form an alliance with non-Moslem rulers of Africa against the Moslems of North Africa. Portugal had had a long and bitter struggle against the Moslems, who had for centuries dominated the Iberian peninsula.

Portugal had succeeded in freeing itself from Moslem domination as far back as 1250, but since that date the Portuguese had from time to time engaged in hostilities against the Moors of the North African coast. In 1415 Prince Henry had taken a leading part in a Portuguese attack on the Moorish stronghold of Ceuta in Morocco. In Henry's time there was a popular legend concerning a Christian king of Africa called Prester John. At one time Prester John was identified with the Christian king of Abyssinia; at other times Prester John's kingdom was said to be located elsewhere on the African continent. Prince Henry had hoped that by sending sailors to the coast of West Africa he could establish contact with Prester John and form an alliance with him to attack the Moslems in North Africa and the Western Sudan.

Secondly, in organizing the voyages of exploration to the coast of West Africa, Prince Henry had the missionary motive of taking the Christian faith to the pagan inhabitants of that part of the African continent. Thirdly, the prince had the twin purpose of seeking adventure and of gaining geographical knowledge of Africa. Knowledge of the geography of Africa was at this time restricted to North Africa with some vague notions of the region of the Red Sea and the East African coast. Lastly Prince Henry had an important economic aim. He desired to gain access from the south to the gold trade of the Western Sudan currently controlled by Moslem North Africa along the trans-Saharan routes. When Henry took part in the Portuguese attack on Ceuta in 1415 he was a young man of twenty-five years. The trans-Saharan gold trade of the Moors was no secret to Europe. The Western Sudan was in fact the principal source of supply of gold to Europe in Prince Henry's time. While at Ceuta he must have met people who knew much about the gold trade of the Moors with the Western Sudan. The middle class merchants of Portugal wished for nothing better than a Portuguese share of the trans-Saharan trade by supplanting the Moors in the Western Sudan from the West African coast to the south. Prince Henry had this very aim in mind.

How far Henry hoped to push Portuguese exploration down the African coast is not clear. It is probable that he waited to see how far chance would carry his sailors on their expeditions. By the end of his life he had most likely begun to cherish hopes of a circumnavigation of Africa or of a sea-way to India.

It is a matter of interest that the Arabs should not have preceded the Portuguese in the exploration of the West Africa coast, for it was from the Arab world that knowledge of many regions of Africa had reached

Europe. At the close of the medieval era, Islamic learning centred in the Arab world was ahead of that of Europe. The mathematical and astro- nomical knowledge which was to help the Portuguese voyages of the fifteenth century were products of the Arab world. Already the Arabs were enjoying prosperous trade with the Western Sudan and they also controlled trade on the Indian Ocean which was virtually an Arab lake. They were carrying on a lucrative trade in precious metals and spices and silks with India and the Far East. They did not appear very interested in pursuing mysteries along the West African coast which might after all lead to little or no profit. Moreover, the Arabs were always fearful about sailing on the Atlantic, which they referred to as 'the Sea of Darkness'. They had decided that this western sea was boundless. Early Arabic writers had regarded it as an expanse of whirlpools and perpetual dark- ness. Any Arab mad enough to wish to attempt to traverse the Atlantic was by law to be deprived of his civic rights.

Progress of the exploration

When Prince Henry established his headquarters at Sagres in 1419, the Canary Islands were already known to Europeans. In 1420 Madeira, which had first become known to Europe in the previous century, was re- discovered by Henry's sailors. There appears to have been some know- ledge of the coast as far as Cape Bojador by the end of the fourteenth century, so that Henry probably knew, before his enterprise began, that the African coast bulged westward beyond that Cape. No one, however, knew about the Gulf of Guinea and the extent of the West African coast.

The first sailors sent out by Prince Henry did not go beyond Cape Nun. It was with great difficulty that Henry's men could be persuaded to sail beyond Cape Bojador. The fears of the Arabs concerning the Atlantic were known and even exaggerated in Europe. The position of Cape Bojador had been known long before Henry organized the Portuguese voyages of exploration; but it was always regarded by sailors with the utmost dread. All sorts of foolish stories were entertained about the coast beyond Bojador. The cape was even held to be 'land's end', beyond which those who ventured farther would fall into a bottomless pit. It was threatened that whoever went beyond it would be scorched black by the burning sun. The region of the cape and beyond was sup- posed to be inhabited by man-eating savages and devils.

In 1433 the Portuguese sea-captain, Gil Eannes, set out determined to sail past Cape Bojador, but he was driven back by empty fears. Prince Henry ordered the captain back to sea with strict instructions to sail

Map 15

beyond the cape. In 1434 Eannes carried out his instructions and did not suffer any of the hideous things commonly held about Bojador. This feat was indeed a turning point in the exploration of the coast of West Africa. After Cape Bojador had been passed, the progress of exploration down the coast was quite steady. In 1435 Rio d'Oro was reached by Gonçalves. The following year Nuno Tristao reached Arguin and a few years later the Portuguese built at that cape their first fort on the West African coast. The Senegal was reached in 1446, followed by the Gambia two years later. Also in 1446 Alvise Ca da Mosto, a Venetian who had accepted service under Henry, reached Cape Verde. Beyond Cape Verde progress of exploration should have quickened, for the inhospitable shores of the Sahara were now behind. In fact further progress was slow. This was because considerable wealth began to be derived from the coast so far explored, and a number of trading ships were being sent out from Portugal to the West African coast.

In 1460 Sierra Leone was reached and so named by Pedro de Cintra. The name Sierra Leone, a later version of the Portuguese *Sierra Lyoa* or 'lion mountain', derives from the fact that the hills rising in the foreground appeared from the shore like wild lions to Pedro de Cintra and his men. Shortly after the discovery of Sierra Leone, Henry the Navigator died. Although a lull followed, the voyages of exploration continued. By the end of 1462 the site of Monrovia in Liberia had been reached.

In 1469 the voyages of exploration were organized on a new basis. The king of Portugal entered into a contract with a rich Lisbon merchant called Fernao Gomez. Gomez was granted a five-year monopoly of the trade of the Guinea Coast in return for an undertaking to explore each year one hundred leagues farther along the coast. In 1471 Pedro de Escabor and Joao de Santarem, two captains in the service of Gomez, reached the Gold Coast, now the Republic of Ghana. The discovery of the Gold Coast was a most important event in the history of Portuguese exploration of the coast of West Africa, for the region was rich in gold. The village of Shama at the mouth of the River Pra became a base for Portuguese trade in the area. In the same year the mouth of the Niger was reached, but the fact that it was the Niger was not realized till well after three hundred years. In 1472 Fernando Po entered the Bight of Biafra and discovered the island that still bears his name. The islands of San Thomé and O Principe in the Bight of Biafra were discovered at about the same time.

In 1474, when Fernao Gomez's contract expired, the Portuguese government would not renew it on account of the discovery of the Gold Coast and the wealth that its gold trade offered. The Portuguese government itself assumed monopoly of the trade of the Guinea Coast. By now the discovery of the entire Guinea Coast may be said to have been completed. However, exploration farther down the coast continued. In 1482 Diego Cao reached the mouth of the Congo and sailed some way up the river. In 1487 Bartholomew Diaz sailed round the Cape of Good Hope and ten years later Vasco da Gama discovered the sea-route to India.

The challenge of the Portuguese monopoly

The discovery of the Gold Coast and the resulting access to abundant gold and the monopoly of trade on the Guinea Coast claimed by the Portuguese aroused the envy and rivalry of other European nations. Not long after the Portuguese had reached the Gold Coast a Flemish ship is said to have reached Elmina. In 1481 there was great alarm in Portugal at the report that an English expedition was being prepared for the Guinea Coast. Portugal made a protest to King Edward IV of England, who appears to have forbidden the proposed expedition. There were Portuguese fears also that seamen from Castile in Spain were contemplating a voyage to the Guinea Coast. The threat to their claim of the monopoly in West Africa prompted the Portuguese to build the first strong fort in Lower Guinea at Elmina.

In December 1481 the King of Portugal commissioned a Portuguese nobleman called Don Diego de Azambuja at the head of an expedition to build a fort at Elmina at the mouth of the small river called Benya. When Azumbuja landed and announced his intention to build a fort, the chief of Elmina and his elders expressed opposition to the project. It was through a mixture of a show of force and promises from the Portuguese that the chief and his people gave in. The name of the chief of Elmina is given in the Portuguese records as Caramansa; this has often been interpreted as Kwamina Ansah. It may be pointed out as a matter of interest that it is by no means clear that the Portuguese negotiated with Kwamina Ansah. Mansa is a Mande word for 'chief' or 'king', a fact already noted when considering the medieval kingdoms of the Western Sudan (Mansa Musa and Mansa Ule, for example).

The fort at Elmina was built with amazing speed and when completed it provided the Portuguese with a strong foothold and defence post in Lower Guinea. It was named Sao Jorge da Mina. In 1486 it was granted the status and privilege of a city by the king of Portugal.

The first European nationals to intervene in the trade of the Guinea Coast were from Castile. King John II of Portugal protested against a number of Castilian expeditions to the coast. However, Castilian seamen continued as serious rivals to the Portuguese on the West African coast until 1492, when Christopher Columbus discovered the New World and opened areas of activities for Spain on the other side of the Atlantic. Frenchmen also began to show interest in the trade of the Guinea Coast during the fifteenth century. In 1492 a French privateer seized a Portuguese caravel laden with gold from the Gold Coast.

In the early years of the sixteenth century the French came forward openly as the principal challengers of the Portuguese in West Africa. Frequent French voyages were made to the coast. Between 1500 and 1530 no less than three hundred Portuguese ships were captured by French raiders along the West African coast. By the middle of the century French ships were visiting the Guinea Coast in considerable numbers. The French showed greater interest in the pepper trade on the Grain Coast than in the slave trade that was steadily developing along the shores of the Gulf of Guinea.

The first English voyage of significance to the Guinea Coast was made in 1553 under Captain Thomas Windham. The English bought some gold in the Elmina area and then sailed eastward to Benin, where they obtained pepper. Many of the English crew lost their lives in the malaria-infested creeks of the Niger delta. Of the one hundred and forty men who had set out on the expedition, only forty lived to return to England. From the commercial point of view, however, the expedition was worthwhile. In the following year another English voyage was made to West Africa under John Lock. In spite of Portuguese hostility, Lock managed to buy some gold at Shama. He returned to England with a rich cargo of gold, ivory and pepper; but he lost twenty-four of his men during the expedition.

In 1561 a number of prominent Englishmen formed a trading partnership called the Company of Merchant Adventurers to Guinea. They made attempts to build forts on the Gold Coast to rival the Portuguese forts there, but without success. Lack of forts on the Guinea Coast compelled the English traders to act as interlopers during the sixteenth century. One of the notable English interlopers was the famous Elizabethan sea captain, John Hawkins, who made a hurried voyage to the Guinea Coast in 1562 and succeeded in carrying a cargo of slaves to the New World.

On the whole neither the French nor the English became well-established on the West African coast in the sixteenth century. The reason for this is not difficult to find. The Portuguese in West Africa were conducting a national enterprise with the full resources of the state of Portugal behind them. The French and the English on the other hand were operating as groups of individual merchants who formed temporary partnerships that were normally dissolved after each voyage. The Portuguese were able throughout the sixteenth century to strengthen their position in West Africa through their many forts along the coast. However, by the end of the sixteenth century the Portuguese were beginning to lose some of their original interest in the trade of the Guinea Coast, largely on account of their more prosperous commercial activities elsewhere in the world, notably in India, the East Indies and Brazil. When the Portuguese were offered a real challenge in West Africa, it came from Holland. In 1580 King Philip II of Spain seized the throne of Portugal. A few years earlier, in 1572, the Dutch had revolted against Spanish rule. Philip II thought he could help his armies in the Netherlands if he forbade the rebellious provinces to trade with the Iberian peninsula. In 1592 he declared this as a policy. The result was other than what Philip had anticipated: the merchants of the Netherlands combined to encroach upon the areas of Portuguese trade overseas.

The first Dutch voyage to West Africa was made about 1593. In 1598 the Dutch made an attack on the island of Fernando Po, where the Portuguese had firmly established themselves. In the same year some Dutch adventurers visited the Gold Coast for the first time and set up small trade posts at a respectful distance from the Portuguese forts. If in the sixteenth century the Dutch intended to make any serious inroad into the Portuguese monopoly of the trade on the Guinea Coast, they failed for the same reason as the French and English attempts of the period.

The Dutch showed greater determination in West Africa in the early decades of the seventeenth century. In 1621 a Dutch West India Company was formed. This company had West Africa in its sphere of activity. Meanwhile the Dutch, following the example by the French and the English, had begun seriously to challenge the Spanish monopoly of the New World by attacking Spanish shipping on the Atlantic. By about 1630 the Dutch had succeeded in seizing control of the Atlantic from Spain, and they proceeded to attack Portuguese possessions in Brazil, a considerable part of which they eventually seized. At this point the Dutch decided to encourage the Portuguese planters in Brazil by supplying them with much-needed slave labour. It was this scheme that rekindled Dutch interest in the Guinea Coast during the first half of the seventeenth century. The Dutch subsequently began a series of attacks on the Portuguese forts and posts on the West African coast. Before the end of the first half of the century they had captured from the Portuguese Arguin and Gorée in Upper Guinea and the island of San Thomé in the Bight of Benin. However, the greatest victory of the Dutch in West Africa occurred in 1637, when they captured from the Portuguese the great fort of Sao Jorge da Mina, where they quickly established their headquarters on the West African coast. In 1642 the Dutch captured the fort at Axim and expelled the Portuguese from the Gold Coast altogether.

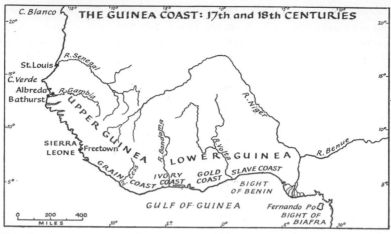

Map 16

Development of trade

The West African coast was divided into two main regions: Upper Guinea and Lower Guinea. The former stretched from Cape Blanco down to Sierra Leone, and the latter from Sierra Leone to the Cameroons. On sailing past Cape Bojador, the Portuguese began to trade with the African tribes living along the coast and in the immediate hinterland. In 1441 some Portuguese sailors returned to Portugal with a small quantity of gold dust and a number of slaves from the Guinea Coast. The wealthy classes of Portugal, who had at first held themselves aloof from Prince Henry's West African adventures, quickly realized that a fortune could be made from the West African coast. Commercial speculation soon began. In 1448 Prince Henry ordered the building of a fort and warehouse on Arguin Island. This was the first European trade post on the coast of West Africa. A few slaves continued to be taken to Portugal where they were employed mainly for domestic service and appear to have been treated quite well by their masters. However, it is an indisputable fact that a new form of trade had begun on the Guinea Coast which was in due course to be associated with great suffering to millions. The Portuguese were soon buying slaves in greater numbers to supply labour on sugar plantations that they had established on the islands of Madeira and the Azores. After exploration of the Guinea Coast was completed, slaves were taken to work on new Portuguese sugar plantations on the islands of San Thomé and Fernando Po.

In general, trade in Upper Guinea centred on a few slaves, gum and a kind of sweet pepper called *malaguetta* or grains of paradise. It was from this kind of pepper that the region of modern Liberia and its neighbourhood derived the name Grain Coast.

After 1448 regular trade was established with the coast south-eastward beyond Cape Verde. Slaves no doubt formed the main commodity, for little gold had so far been found in Upper Guinea. In due course some ivory was obtained from the coast still known as the Ivory Coast, but the Portuguese do not appear to have shown much interest in ivory, possibly because the principal markets for it were in the Levant with which the Portuguese could not easily trade.

When Gomez obtained the contract to trade on the Guinea Coast in 1469 in return for continued exploration of the coast farther east, his men made it their policy to trade as quickly as possible wherever they touched on the coast and then sail away. On the Ivory Coast, where they found the inhabitants not readily inclined to trade, they formed the habit of kidnapping persons they chanced to lay hands on. After 1471 the Gold Coast became the main centre of commercial activity on the Guinea Coast on account of the abundance of gold to be had. After the Portuguese fort of Sao Jorge da Mina had been built at Elmina, King John II of Portugal began to make territorial claims in West Africa. He assumed the title Lord of Guinea which, however, carried little substance.

The Portuguese established contact with the inland city-state of Benin as early as 1485. Pepper was the main article of trade but later slaves were bought in ever-growing numbers. The Bini (as the people of Benin are called) were waging frequent wars on their neighbours and thus had captives on hand to sell to the Portuguese as slaves. At first the Portuguese used Gwato as a port to Benin but later they established themselves on the island of San Thomé. In the sixteenth and seventeenth centuries the English and the Dutch challenged the Portuguese monopoly of trade in the Bights of Benin and Biafra, just as they were doing on the coast of the Gold Coast. There was active European trade in the Niger delta to the east of Benin. Some palm oil was exported from the numerous creeks that eventually came to be known as the Oil Rivers. In due course, however, the slave trade rivalled and overshadowed the trade in oil.

The most active scene of European trade on the West African coast in the sixteenth and seventeenth centuries was the Gold Coast. The trade in gold here was of particular importance to the European traders. The tribes both on the coast and in the interior responded readily to the

F

growing trade with the Europeans. The European forts that dotted the coast bear testimony to the value the Europeans placed on trade in the region. The forts served as protected residence for the European merchants as well as warehouses for the goods they brought to West Africa. As the slave trade gradually assumed greater dimensions the forts served as depots for storing slaves until the arrival of the slave ships that would take them on the voyage across the Atlantic to the New World. East of the Gold Coast the European traders did not as a rule resort much to forts in conducting trade: they contented themselves with building small trade posts. In the lagoons and creeks that abound on the coast to the east, the European traders maintained special depots for slaves called *barracoons*. For many years after the Portuguese voyages of exploration, the Dahomeyan coast was virtually by-passed because it had no article of commercial value to offer the Europeans, but after the middle of the seventeenth century it became one of the principal centres of supply of slaves and actually earned the name Slave Coast.

The various European nationals who visited the coast of West Africa during this period conducted their trade mainly from their forts, factories and other posts on the coast, making little or no effort to penetrate inland. In Upper Guinea the Portuguese made some attempts to reach the tribes inland but the results were not often rewarding. In 1487 they built a trade post at Wadan in the hinterland of Cape Blanco, but it was soon abandoned. Individual Portuguese efforts were made to reach Timbuktu in the Western Sudan. Portuguese traders penetrated into the Gambia and Senegal with varying degrees of success. In the main the Portuguese chose to conduct their trade (except on the Gold Coast, where they had forts) from off-shore islands, notably Arguin and the Cape Verde Islands and San Thomé and Fernando Po in the Gulf of Guinea.

Survey of the trans-Atlantic slave trade

Introduction

Slavery was a recognized social institution in Africa long before the Europeans appeared on the shores of West Africa; but slavery is not the same thing as the slave trade. Captives made in the tribal wars of pre-colonial Africa were sometimes put to domestic service or labour in the fields. Persons condemned in the courts of chiefs for crimes and mis-demeanour might end up by finding themselves reduced to a status like that of slaves. On the whole, however, slavery in old Africa can be claimed to have been void of undue hardship. A good deal of slavery in old Africa can be classified as domestic slavery: the slave was to all intents and purposes regarded as a member of his master's family. In most cases he could own property and was by custom and practice protected against extreme cruelty and injustice. A female slave could become the wife of her master. When this happened to her, she virtually ceased to be a slave any more, and any children she might bear were free-born. A male slave could marry a daughter or a close relative of his master's. If a slave gave good service and behaved himself he could be declared a free man at the will of his master. Slaves are known to have succeeded to the property of their masters even to the exclusion of the masters' children. Certainly not all slaves could end up in such fortunate circumstances. Many must have remained obscure until their death; and some would undoubtedly suffer some injustice and indignity. The temptation to make a slave a victim in human sacrifice must at times have been irresistible. However, on the whole it would be a great error not to differentiate between the domestic slavery of old Africa and the slave trade conducted by and through the instigation of foreigners.

It may be observed that although it was at the hands of Europeans that West Africa suffered from the slave trade, in other parts of the continent trade in slaves existed long before the coming of the Europeans. For centuries North African merchants had taken African slaves from the Western Sudan to North Africa and the Orient. The trans-Saharan trade routes that linked North Africa and the Sudan were strewn with the skeletons of thousands of African slaves who perished during the long marches across the desert.

Before attempting a brief survey of the trans-Atlantic slave trade, it may be worth while to warn the reader against developing unduly hostile passion towards those who participated in the harmful trade. In other words, he would be well advised not to fall into the common temptation of judging the men who bought and sold slaves outside the moral standards and circumstances of their times. The Europeans who bought slaves from Africa for two or three centuries after the Portuguese voyages of exploration did not view the slave trade in the same light that progressive people viewed it later. This is important. First of all, it should be recognized that the period of the trans-Atlantic slave trade was not, generally speaking, an age in which the concept of humanity and human dignity was universally accepted. Even in Western European countries supposed to be the most advanced, such as England, dreadful brutalities were practised on nationals. Prisoners were brutally treated; women and young children were exploited in industries in most shocking ways. Writers who published disagreeable material were pilloried and flogged. Hanging and whipping of criminals and common offenders in public were frequent. When these happened they were occasions for amusement for the general public. Men of such temperament could hardly be expected to show much feeling towards slaves of another race. Secondly it may be pointed out that those who profited by the slave trade – merchants and plantation owners – saw the slave trade as just another form of commercial enterprise. Slaves were regarded as an ordinary commodity and the property of their owners. Without meaning any particular censure to them, it may be observed that, by and large, the old-established Christian churches did not always feel too strongly about the slave trade, although they were sometimes worried about its rigors and the suffering of its victims. Finally, it should be recorded in fairness that it was not all slave owners and traders who practised brutalities on their slaves. Many slave owners and planters, if not for the sake of humanity, at least in the interest of pure economics, thought it wise to show interest in the welfare of their slaves.

Beginnings of the slave trade

Shortly after the Portuguese had reached Upper Guinea they began to buy African slaves. The first slaves reached Portugal in 1442. They were mainly employed in domestic service and appear to have been fairly well treated. Their first arrival in Portugal, however, was a sad occasion. Azurara has recorded in his *Chronicles of Guinea* an eye-witness account of the arrival of some of the early African slaves in Portugal: 'What heart was that, how hard so ever, which was not pierced with sorrow seeing that company; for some had sunken cheeks and their faces bathed in tears, looking at each other, others were groaning very bitterly . . .; others struck their faces with their hands, throwing themselves on the earth; others made their loneliness in songs, according to the customs of their country which corresponded well to the height of their sorrow'.

As the Portuguese sailed farther down the coast of West Africa, they continued to carry more and more African slaves to Europe. But all told the number of slaves that reached Europe bears no comparison whatsoever with the great trans-Atlantic slave trade which had its origins in circumstances connected with the discovery of the New World. In 1492 Christopher Columbus, financed and supported by King Ferdinand and Queen Isabella of Spain, reached the West Indies in his venture to reach the Far East by sailing progressively westward. Soon afterwards the

mainland of a new continent, to become known as America, was discovered. Spain quickly claimed the lands of the New World and Spanish
adventurers flocked to the West Indies and the mainland to seek quick
fortune. The first attraction in the New World was gold and precious
metals in general, but when the amount of this form of treasure had
finally dwindled, the disillusioned fortune-hunters turned to the rich soil
of the West Indian islands for tropical crops, first sugar-cane and later
cotton and tobacco. In the early decades of the sixteenth century the
Spaniards discovered rich deposits of silver and gold on the South
American mainland and the crave for quick wealth grew apace. Whether
they turned to agriculture on the West Indian islands or to mining on the
mainland, the one great problem that faced the Spaniards was labour to
exploit the natural resources of the New World.

   The Spaniards were unwilling to work themselves to gain the wealth
they were after. At first they attempted to use the native 'Indians' for
both farming and mining, but the result was disastrous. These Indians
were an easy-going race who were totally unaccustomed to hard work
for which they had never felt the need in any case. Queen Isabella as ruler
of Castile in her own right was opposed to her Spanish subjects in the
New World enslaving the Indians and forcing them to work for them.
However, she later reluctantly permitted herself to be won over by the
argument that the Indians must be compelled to work if they were to have
contact with the Spaniards and become civilized. The plight of the
Indians under Spanish forced labour aroused the pity and sympathy of a
Spanish priest called Las Casas who had gone to the New World shortly
after its discovery. He owned a plantation and some Indian slaves whom
he treated well. But soon the misery and suffering of Indian slaves in
general convinced Las Casas that slavery was bad for the Indians.
Between 1515 and 1517 Las Casas fought unsuccessfully to prevent the
rulers of Spain from enslaving Indians in the New World. As a sub-
stitute for Indian slaves Las Casas suggested the importation of African
slaves from the coast of West Africa into the New World. The African
was robust and much stronger than the Indian. The African was thus
regarded as being admirably suited for the kind of labour needed on the
plantations and in the mines in the New World. The African lived in a
climate similar to that of the West Indies. Moreover, it was said that he
was capable of doing the work of four Indians. And so the idea of
transporting African slaves across the Atlantic ocean to the New World
began for practical reasons. Las Casas no doubt had offered the
suggestion in good faith and in an effort to prevent the Indians from

dying off like flies, as they were doing under the slave-yoke of Spanish forced labour; but he lived long enough to witness the plight of African slaves also in the New World and to regret his suggestion. However, there appeared to be no other alternative. The discovery of the New World and the economic possibilities which opened up there led to three centuries of the trans-Atlantic slave trade, one of the greatest tragedies in human history.

The organization of the slave trade

By a proclamation made by the Pope and known as the Papal Bull of Demarcation (later modified by the Treaty of Tordesillas) there was fixed an imaginary line running north to south, 270 leagues west of the Azores which divided the new discoveries of the fifteenth century between Spain and Portugal. The lands west of the line belonged to Spain and those to the east fell under Portuguese domain. Thus while the New World, which required cheap slave labour to exploit its resources lay in the Spanish sphere, the west coast of Africa, from where the slaves were expected to come, lay in the Portuguese zone. The Portuguese were not keen on carrying African slaves to the New World, nor was the Spanish Government desirous of intruding into the Portuguese con-trolled West African coast. Spain resorted to the device of granting special licences to individuals to supply the Spanish colonies in America with African slaves. Two situations arose in this connection. First the licensed suppliers were totally unable to cope with the ever-growing demand for African slaves in the New World. Secondly the supply of slaves quickly became such a lucrative business that interlopers, that is people without a licence, began to carry slaves from Africa to the Spanish American colonies. By the middle of the seventeenth century those supplying slaves without a licence had become so active that one Spanish licence-holder complained to the king of Spain that for every hundred Negroes brought openly to Hispaniola, two hundred were introduced secretly. Sir John Hawkins was the first Englishman of note to appear in the trans-Atlantic slave trade as an interloper. In 1562 he appeared on the coast of Sierra Leone and took to America three hundred slaves he had 'got into his possession partly by the sword and partly by other means'. He sold his cargo secretly to Spanish colonists in America at a great profit.

The issue of licences to individuals to supply African slaves to the Spanish colonies proved unsatisfactory on account of the inadequacy of supplies. Spain now began to grant licences not to individuals but to foreign governments. This kind of concession became known as an *Asiento*. It was first offered to the Dutch, followed by the French. In 1713, under the Treaty of Utrecht, England obtained the contract 'to supply the Spanish colonies in America with a total of 144,000 Negro slaves over a period of thirty years, with an added right to supply further slaves as and when they might be desired'. The trans-Atlantic slave trade benefited three different parties: the colonists in America, the buyers and carriers of African slaves across the ocean and the Africans who obtained and sold slaves to the Europeans on the Guinea Coast.

On the coast of West Africa itself the collection and sale of slaves was well organized. Along the coast, notably on the Gold Coast, European merchants of various nationalities maintained forts which served among other things as depots for receiving and keeping the slaves before the slave ships came to carry them to the New World. Elsewhere on the Guinea Coast, and the Slave Coast (from Dahomey to the Cameroons) few European forts were built. The numerous creeks and lagoons along this part of the West African coast afforded the slave merchants sufficient protection and facilitated the collection of slaves from centres maintained by African middlemen.

The majority of the slaves came from the interior. On the coast were African middlemen who effected the transaction between the slave traders and the European slave buyers. In the early years of the trade, European nationals practised the kidnapping of unwary Africans, but it met with great hostility from the local people. The experience of the Englishman John Lock serves as an illustration. In 1554 Lock kidnapped five men and carried them away as slaves. The act proved dangerous to the position of the English as merchants in the area. They had been hitherto favoured by the Africans because, unlike the Portuguese and the Spaniards, the English had not indulged in kidnapping. The Africans now decided not to sell gold and ivory to any English merchant. The other English merchants were so alarmed that they prevailed upon Lock to return the five men to the coast from where they had been kidnapped. After the return of the unfortunate victims the English 'regained their reputation and their innocent trade'.

Not only was the kidnapping of slaves by the Europeans themselves undesirable; as a source of supply it must have been most erratic and extremely limited. No doubt the European merchants quickly settled down to persuading the chiefs on the coast to sell criminals and prisoners into slavery. Finding the business of selling slaves a lucrative one, the chiefs would be tempted to use all sorts of pretexts to sell more and more of their hapless subjects. Foreigners and poor travellers not on their guard were liable to be surprised and carried off into slavery. When the local source of supply ran out, the chiefs and men who had acquired the taste for European goods in exchange for slaves would naturally look farther afield for the supply of slaves. As the demand for slaves increased, ruthless methods were used to meet it. The most cruel and wasteful method was by slave raids, by which armed gangs surrounded helpless villages, carrying away the youth and the able-bodied and leaving behind them ruin and misery. If the scene of a slave raid was near the coast, in the vicinity of the fort or barracoon, the captives had an easier lot before being sold into slavery. If they were captured a long way from the coast, the long march to the sea could be disastrous. The reader will no doubt be familiar with the common story of the march of misery. Exhaustion, hunger, thirst and disease killed many captives before they reached the slave market and the depots. Over wide areas in the interior of West Africa, society was dislocated as a result of slave raids and wars were waged with the main aim of making captives for the slave market.

Effects of the slave trade
It has been roughly estimated that during the three hundred years of the slave trade, between fifteen to twenty million slaves were carried away from West Africa to the New World. The majority of the slaves were taken from the Gold Coast, Dahomey, Nigeria and the Cameroons. A similar number is estimated to have perished at various stages between the raids and wars in the interior and the passage across the Atlantic. For every slave that arrived safely in the New World, another is believed to have lost his life. All told, therefore, West Africa lost between thirty and forty millions of its population in the course of the slave trade. This is a staggering figure, but it should be borne in mind that this loss was spread over three centuries. This works out an average annual loss of between 100,000 to 130,000. The volume of the trade varied from place to place and from century to century. What made the loss a serious blow to West Africa is not so much the numerical size as the fact that it was usually the youth and the able-bodied upon whom the economy depended who were carried away. Whatever view one takes of the effect of the slave trade on the population of West Africa, there can be little doubt that the trade brought with it untold misery to thousands of people over wide ranges of this part of Africa.

The flight of people from their villages and the general destruction to life and property during slave raids created utter confusion in the areas affected. Even where it became possible for fugitives to return to their deserted abodes, the loss of the young men and women taken away into captivity seriously affected the economy and social life in many parts of the interior. The constant expectation of raids and destruction led to a general state of uncertainty in which planning and forward-looking policies became meaningless. Civilized and improved conditions of living rest upon stability. The slave raids removed the basis of settled life and thus halted or even destroyed the prerequisite for the orderly development of human progress. The ruin that was likely to be done to agriculture by slave raids and wars could cause food shortages and create famine.

Although the Africans who raided and sold slaves made material gains in the traffic, they were losers in the moral sense. Men who acted with such ruthlessness as the slave raids demanded were likely to become brutalized in causing the misery that they consciously or unconsciously spread. The neighbourliness and fellow-feeling for which the African is proverbially known must have suffered a set-back in the brutalities of the slave trade. The development of African art and craft was likely to suffer a decline in the circumstance of the slave trade. The capturing and selling of slaves was a profitable pursuit which could tempt the craftsman to give up his skill for the new quick way of making profit. Increased trade with Europeans in any form involving an influx of mass-produced goods was bound to adversely affect African home industries; but the sad thing about the deterioration of African art and craft during the period of the slave trade is that West Africa was paying for European goods not by means of productive activity but by the negative process of slave hunting.

Some writers have drawn attention to the fact that those regions that suffered most from the slave trade are among the most densely populated and the most advanced states of West Africa today. This is interesting but hardly any tangible conclusions may be drawn from this fact. Other writers have expressed doubt if West Africa could have developed its agriculture to produce enough food to sustain a growing population undepleted by the slave trade. This view hardly makes a case. There is so much fruitful but uncultivated land in West Africa today that such fears and doubts appear groundless.

The slave trade is claimed to have aided the emergence of certain states in West Africa. Asante, Dahomey, Benin and Oyo certainly gained wealth from the slave trade. Wealth helps to build and develop states,

F*

but care is needed in evaluating the relationship between the slave trade and the development of states in the Guinea forest. All four West African states mentioned above had already emerged as states before they became involved in the slave trade, except perhaps Dahomey to some extent. It is interesting to note that all the four states which are claimed to have emerged through their activities in the slave trade declined and subsequently disintegrated in the end, largely on account of their obsession with the slave trade. What the slave trade might have given to these states with one hand it took away with the other. On balance it is quite clear that the slave trade acted as a factor that retarded the orderly progress of West Africa.

The Europeans in West Africa during the seventeenth and eighteenth centuries

During the seventeenth and eighteenth centuries, trade on the Guinea Coast, especially the lucrative trade in slaves, attracted a considerable number of European nationals. The English, Dutch, French, Swedes, Danes and Germans (Brandenburghers) all tried with varying degrees of success to establish trade posts and spheres of influence along the West African coast after the end of the monopoly of the Portuguese and their expulsion from the coast. On the whole, however, it was the English, French and Dutch who dominated the scene.

The French

In the seventeenth and eighteenth centuries Upper Guinea was the principal scene of French commercial activity and influence in West Africa. In the 1630s they established trade posts at the mouth of the Senegal which they found to be a valuable waterway into the interior. In 1659 they set up their headquarters on the island of St. Louis on the river. In 1677 they succeeded in capturing from the Dutch Arguin and Gorée which the Dutch themselves had snatched earlier from the Portuguese. Steadily the French strengthened their position in Upper Guinea. Between 1664 and 1758 no less than six French companies were set up successively (each after the financial failure of its predecessor) to develop trade in Upper Guinea, especially on the Senegal.

French enterprise in Upper Guinea received remarkable stimulus under the direction of an energetic Frenchman named André Brue between 1697 and 1720. In Brue's time a French company operating along the Senegal concluded treaties with the Fula, Soninke and other related peoples living along the river. Eventually French traders and adventurers reached Bambuk, the famed gold-bearing region of Wangara of the medieval Western Sudan. To the south of the Senegal Brue developed Albreda on the Gambia. The French established trade posts at Bisao and Bulama after a successful invasion of the country later to be known as Portuguese Guinea.

The French traded in ivory, hides, slaves, wax and gum in Upper Guinea, but on the whole their profits were not satisfactory considering the amount of capital and zeal put into the development of trade. The unsatisfactory returns and the eventual failure of French commercial enterprise may be attributed first, to overestimation of the possibilities for the development of trade on the part of the various French companies and, secondly, to the fact that Upper Guinea as a whole did not produce enough of the most lucrative article of trade in West Africa at the time, namely, slaves. Later the French found it necessary to transfer their slave trading activities to the so-called Slave Coast, in particular to Dahomey. Towards the end of the seventeenth century they tried to develop trade on the Ivory Coast. They established a trade post at Half Assini but had to abandon it shortly afterwards in 1705.

One of André Brue's successors, Pierre David, tried between 1736 and 1746 to continue Brue's policy of expansion of French influence inland along the Senegal. He attempted to bring about understanding between the French and the English who were in the process of developing their own trade on the Gambia. This policy seems to have enjoyed a measure of success until the Seven Years War (1756–63) during which the English and the French were engaged in a bitter struggle for supremacy in India and North America. Brue's French empire in West Africa dwindled. During the Seven Years War the English captured nearly all the French posts in Upper Guinea. At the Treaty of Paris in 1763, which concluded the war, Gorée was returned to the French, but the English retained the other French posts they had captured.

The English
From the seventeenth century the English spread their trading activities along the Guinea Coast in general but the Senegal-Gambia region was one of their main centres. English trade in Upper Gambia was not, however, as valuable as the trade on the Gold Coast. In the Senegal-Gambia region and on the Gold Coast the English were drawn into the affairs of the local peoples more than at any other points of the West African coast except perhaps in Sierra Leone during the last decades of the eighteenth century.

During the second half of the sixteenth century the coast between the Senegal and Gambia Rivers was already the scene of a number of English expeditions. English merchants based in Exeter had obtained the permission of Queen Elizabeth I in 1588 to trade in the area. Then in the early seventeenth century English traders and adventurers began to sail up the Gambia in an attempt to develop trade with the peoples of its banks. In 1620 two Englishmen, Thompson and Jobson, sailed for some 600 miles up the river trying to learn about it and to establish contact with the inhabitants of the areas through which it flowed. An English trading company formed in 1660 under the name Royal Adventurers Trading to Africa succeeded in securing a foothold at James Fort on an island on the Gambia. The Royal Africa Company, which succeeded the Royal Adventurers in 1672, conducted a careful survey of the river.

Throughout this period the English had to struggle against the French and the Dutch who were also cultivating commercial interests and influence in Upper Guinea along the Senegal as well as the Gambia. It has already been noted that in 1677 the French captured Arguin and Gorée from the Dutch. The struggle for the control of trade in Upper Guinea was henceforth between the English and the French.

The Crown Colony of Senegambia
It has already been pointed out that during the Seven Years War the English captured practically all the French posts in Upper Guinea. As a consequence of the Treaty of Paris in 1763 the English returned only Gorée to the French. In the following year the English embarked upon an interesting colonial experiment in West Africa. They added the French posts in their hands to their own posts in the Gambia which had hitherto been administered by the Company of Merchants, to constitute the Crown Colony of Senegambia.

Senegambia was given a constitution which provided for a Royal Governor, a nominated council and an elaborate system of courts of justice. To finance the colony it was hoped that ample revenue could be obtained from a levy on trade in the area. However, the whole experiment of Senegambia failed for two main reasons. In the first place the new form of government and administrative arrangements imposed upon the inhabitants of the colony were entirely outside their experience and thus proved unworkable. Secondly the colony was unable to raise the revenue necessary for effective administration and the provision of public services. It was poor judgement on the part of the English to have returned Gorée to the French, for Gorée became a centre for the evasion of payment of duty on trade imposed by the government of Senegambia. British difficulties during the War of American Independence (1778–83) finally killed off Senegambia as a colonial experiment. During the war the French, who had taken sides with the rebellious American colonies against Britain, recaptured St. Louis and most of their former posts in Upper Guinea. Although the British were able to capture Gorée during the hostilities, at the Peace of Versailles in 1783 they lost their former holdings in Upper Guinea except the posts in the Gambia. After the collapse of the Crown Colony of Senegambia the Gambia was restored to the control of the Company of Merchants.

The Colony of Sierra Leone
English traders were active in Sierra Leone from the beginning of the seventeenth century. The various English trading associations that operated in West Africa – the Company of London Merchants, the Company of Royal Adventurers and the Royal African Company – all tried to develop trade on the coast of Sherbo, Tasso and Bunce Islands and built a few forts. However, English trade on this section of the West African coast does not appear to have been very prosperous and in fact trade showed a definite decline towards the end of the seventeenth century. In the last two decades of the century English trade in Sierra Leone came under disquieting attacks by the French privateers. Sierra Leone was a favourite haunt for interlopers. The officials of the English companies trading in Sierra Leone, especially those of the Royal African Company, hindered the fortunes of their employers by forming the notorious habit of cheating and trading privately on their own account.
   Even in the face of such difficulties British merchants still clung to the coast of Sierra Leone in the eighteenth century as they had done in the previous one. The most remarkable British achievement in Sierra Leone came during the second half of the eighteenth century with the establishment of a settlement for displaced people of African descent and freed slaves whose growing presence in England was creating a serious social problem. It was customary for English planters in the New World returning to England on leave or final retirement to take along with them their domestic slaves. One such slave refused to return with his master to the New World. The master eventually brought his runaway slave before an English court in 1772. The judge, Lord Mansfield, freed the runaway slave, ruling that 'the status of slavery is so odious that nothing can support it but a positive law' and that the moment a slave set foot on English soil he became a free person. Thousands of slaves who had been brought to

England consequently became free. The numbers of these former slaves were swollen by the arrival in England of many more Negroes who had fought on the side of Britain during the War of American Independence and who did not wish to remain in the United States when its independence was recognized. These men did not fit well into English life and the question of their settlement caught the imagination of abolitionists, especially Granville Sharp. In the end it was decided to settle them somewhere in Africa, and Sierra Leone was suggested as a possible place.

The British Government provided free transport and stores for the expatriation of about 450 Negroes to Sierra Leone as a beginning of the project of resettlement. The expedition was placed in the charge of a naval officer, Captain Thompson. A piece of land was acquired for the settlers at the mouth of the Sierra Leone River and a camp was set up for them at the part of the river called the Watering Place. This rough settlement was called Granville Town after the benevolent Granville Sharp. The whole programme of settlement was attended by a series of misfortunes. For one thing preparations for the settlement were inadequate and one disaster followed another. Disease had broken out on board ship, claiming many lives before the expedition could reach Sierra Leone. The site chosen by Captain Thompson for the settlement was unhealthy, and the arrival of the settlers during the rainy season made matters worse. Before Thompson left the coast after four months, nearly ninety of the settlers had died.

Granville Sharp came to the help of the unfortunate settlers by sending them more supplies. Meanwhile a dispute had arisen over the acquisition of land for the settlement. A sub-chief called King Tom had signed a treaty granting the 'piece of land to the settlers for the sum of £59. But King Tom's overlord, by name Naimbana, insisted on a new treaty. In the end Naimbana received another £85 worth of goods before signing the new treaty granting the land to the settlers officially. This treaty, signed on 22 August 1788, is said to mark the legal beginning of the colony of Sierra Leone.

It was to take much time and money before the settlement could establish itself, but the English Government was not prepared to spend money on development of the settlement. In the end it was proposed to finance the settlement from the profits of a trading company to be set up to develop legitimate trade as opposed to the slave trade in the interior of West Africa. In 1791 the Sierra Leone Company was subsequently launched by an Act of the British Parliament to administer the land acquired from Naimbana. A new and healthier site was chosen for the settlement. This became known as Freetown.

In the following years the population of Freetown grew apace. The first substantial addition to the population came from the British Colony of Nova Scotia north of the United States of America. During the course of the American War of Independence many African slaves freed by the British army came under the protection of the British. These were later taken to Nova Scotia and promised their permanent freedom as well as lands for farming. However, years passed and many of them did not receive the promised farms. When winter came they suffered terribly from the bitter cold. One of the disappointed men, by name Thomas Peters, managed to reach England, where he revealed the plight of his fellow freed slaves. In the end the directors of the newly formed Sierra Leone Company agreed to find a new home for the Africans in Nova Scotia in Sierra Leone. In January 1792, 1,190 of them set sail from Nova Scotia for Sierra Leone to join the new settlement at Freetown. The arrival of the men from Nova Scotia brought new life to the Sierra Leone Colony, for the new arrivals made good settlers: they were sturdy, hard-working men and keen Christians. But even these Nova Scotians had their trials: many of them died after falling ill not long after their arrival in West Africa. Those who survived were given lands not at the Watering Place but in-land in the mountains rising behind Freetown.

New arrivals to the colony also came from the West Indian island of Jamaica. A number of runaway slaves, many of whom were said to be Asante from the Gold Coast, had during the seventeenth century established a state of their own in the mountains of Jamaica. They had succeeded in beating off repeated attempts by the Jamaican Govern-ment to overcome them. They were known as the Maroons. In 1795 the Maroons were at last overpowered by the government, thanks to the use of fierce dogs against them. They were shipped together with their wives and children to Nova Scotia. They too suffered from the bitter cold of winter and it became necessary to settle them elsewhere. The English Government finally decided to settle them in the colony of Sierra Leone.

The new colony of Sierra Leone had many teething troubles. Although the settlers were of African origin, Africa was a strange place to them. Moreover, they did not take readily to hard work which alone could lay the foundation of future prosperity for the colony. The administration that was set up was hardly effective, as the governor and the council provided to help him quarrelled about authority. The law-courts set up by the Sierra Leone Company were not respected by the settlers who also refused to pay rent to the company in respect of plots of land allocated to them. They developed notions about who should run the government of the colony. The trading activities of the company did not go well, for so widespread was the slave trade that considerable time was needed to develop legitimate trade in the interior. The French further confounded an already confused state of affairs by attacking and burning down the colony in 1794. The whole experiment of the colony of Sierra Leone was probably saved by the fortunate appointment of Zachary Macaulay as Governor in 1794. Macaulay handled the settlers carefully and wisely and won their confidence by inviting them to share in the making of laws. In 1800, a year after Macaulay had departed on serving his term as governor, a serious revolt organized by a minority of dissatisfied settlers threatened the colony. Happily in the same year the British Government decided to make a subsidy to cover the expenses of running the colony. In 1808 company rule came to an end and Sierra Leone was declared a British Crown Colony.

English and Dutch on the Gold Coast

In 1637 the Dutch captured the fort of Sao Jorge at Elmina from the Portuguese and finally drove them away from Ghana in 1642. For the next two hundred years or more the struggle for monopoly of the trade of the Gold Coast was between the English and the Dutch (Map 17).

By the close of the sixteenth century the only European posts on the Gold Coast were four Portuguese forts at Axim, Shama, Elmina and Accra. By the end of the eighteenth century the Dutch controlled eleven forts, the British eight, and the Danes one. The Swedes and the Brandenburghers also had a few posts for a short while. The forts ranged from Keta near the Volta in the east to Axim near the Ankobra in the west. They changed hands as the fortunes of the various European companies trading on the coast rose and fell from time to time. During the first half of the seventeenth century British trade on the Gold Coast was conducted by two companies under royal charter. The Company of Adventurers of London Trading into Africa, established in 1618, was followed on its collapse by another chartered company set up in 1631. This second chartered company was meant to rival the Dutch West India Company established in about 1629.

The First Anglo-Dutch War of 1651–4 affected the position of the English and Dutch merchants on the Gold Coast. At the time the English had only one fort at Kormantine and they found it difficult to hold their own against the Dutch with their strong forts at Axim, Butri, Sekondi,

Shama and Mori, besides the magnificent castle at Elmina. Although peace was made between England and Holland in 1654, hostilities between the merchants of the two countries continued on the Guinea Coast.

In 1662 the English trade on the Gold Coast was reorganized with the formation of the Company of Royal Adventurers of England Trading to Africa. This company was granted a royal charter to trade from the Straits of Gibraltar to the Cape of Good Hope, so it was not only concerned with trade on the Gold Coast. It was to supply 3,000 slaves each year to the West Indies. The new company took over the fort at Kormantine and quickly built other forts and lodges at Anashan, Egya, Komenda and Winneba in addition to the famous Cape Coast Castle (1662–3). This amounted to a serious challenge of the monopoly of the trade in West Africa which the Dutch claimed to have acquired from the Portuguese whom they had ousted in 1642. The Dutch resorted to inciting the local people against the English but they did not always succeed in harming the position the English had attained by the building of forts and lodges.

During the Second Anglo-Dutch War (1665–6) the English Government sent Captain Robert Holmes with a fleet to the West African Coast. Holmes lost no time in taking the Dutch forts at Shama, Mori and Anomabu. But this action served merely as a raid, because Holmes returned to England without leaving men behind to garrison the Dutch forts which he had taken, nor did he strengthen the English ones. The Government of Holland ordered the Dutch Admiral de Ruyter on duty off Gibraltar to move quickly with his fleet of thirteen ships to the West African coast and in particular to the Gold Coast to restore the Dutch forts captured by Holmes. De Ruyter swiftly fulfilled his mission and seized from the English merchants control of the forts and other trade posts at Takoradi, Anashan, Kormantine, Komenda, Winneba, Shama, Mori and Anomabu. The English were left in possession only of their magnificent castle at Cape Coast which De Ruyter was unwilling to risk attacking, although he was urged by the Dutch merchants to do so as a final blow to the English. Unlike Holmes, De Ruyter garrisoned the forts and posts he had taken from the English, thus making it difficult for the English to recapture them.

The Treaty of Breda which ended the Second Anglo-Dutch War left the English merchants on the Gold Coast with only Cape Coast Castle. This, however, did not discourage English commercial enterprise on the Gold Coast. In 1672 a new company called the Royal African Company

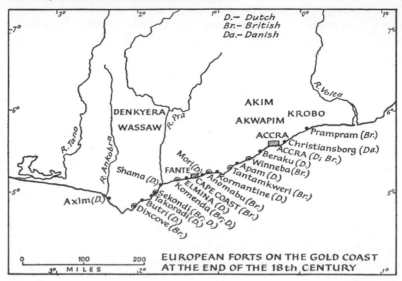

Map 17

was formed, and it entered heart and soul into the slave trade which was becoming ever more lucrative. Between 1680 and 1700 an estimated 140,000 slaves from West Africa were taken to the New World by this company.

The Royal African Company bought Cape Coast Castle and built James Fort at Accra in 1673 and two other forts at Komenda and Anomabu. The Royal African Company seems to have got off to a good start, for apart from the trade in slaves it is said that it was able to send to England 'a great quantity of gold, from which the first guineas were struck by the (English) Mint'.

A glance at the map will show that the British and Dutch forts between Axim and Accra were interspersed almost evenly with the result that the merchants of the two nations were always treading on the toes of each other. The pity of it is that the struggle between the British and the Dutch led to bitterness and intrigue among the local people who supported the one and those who supported the other of the two merchant groups. For example, the people of Elmina backed and encouraged by the Dutch developed a long-standing feud with the people of Komenda who enjoyed the support of the British. British and Dutch rivalry for trade on the Gold Coast continued far into the nineteenth century when the Dutch were compelled to leave the coast in complete control of the British.

The Dahomeyan and Nigerian coasts
The coastline between the mouth of the Volta and Lagos had received only scant attention by the Portuguese as well as the other European traders who came to West Africa during the sixteenth century. From their island headquarters of San Thomé in the Bight of Benin, the Portuguese had during the sixteenth century exchanged cotton goods, corals and iron for local cloth, peppers and ivory with the inhabitants of the Dahomeyan coast, but Portuguese trade here does not appear to have been considerable. The Slave Coast, as this section of the Guinea Coast was called, had no gold and was generally considered to be disappointing by European traders during the sixteenth century. No factories were built on the Dahomeyan coast during this period.

From the middle of the seventeenth century, however, the neglected coastline came into the limelight. The demand for slaves to work on the expanding plantations in the New World was almost insatiable. The English, French and Dutch now began to show considerable interest in the coast of Dahomey and farther east as a reliable source of supply of slaves. By the end of the seventeenth century the English, French and Dutch had established trade relations with Allah and Whydah on the Dahomeyan coast. The European merchants built a few trade posts in Dahomey, but such posts were different from those on the Gold Coast. In Dahomey the European trade posts or factories, as they were called, were usually humble structures of mud and thatch which the kings and magnates in Dahomey insisted should be built miles inland and not on the coast. This precaution was to avoid the experience on the Gold Coast where the European merchants were using their stone forts and castles erected right on the shore to dominate and overawe the local peoples.

Although the kingdom of Dahomey with its inland capital of Abomey was able to supply considerable numbers of slaves to the European traders, the Dutch, French and English companies engaged in the slave trade on the Dahomeyan coast do not appear to have done very successful business, except possibly the Dutch East India Company. The coastline with its numerous lagoons and creeks was ideal for the privateer and the interloper who conducted his trade stealthily and quickly, and set off with no overhead expenses to think about as the organized trading companies had to do. The English Royal African Company was plunged into debt before the end of the seventeenth century. In the first half of the eighteenth century the company could maintain its fort at Whydah only by means of a subsidy which it received from the English Government. It eventually wound up its business in

Dahomey and the control of its fort passed to the Company of Merchants Trading to West Africa. Similarly two French companies, the West India Company and the Guinea Company, could not fare better than the English companies on the Dahomeyan coast.

From the second decade of the eighteenth century the slave trade reached its peak on the coast of Dahomey. It has been claimed that the French were exporting nearly 6,000 slaves a year, the English and the Portuguese nearly 7,000 together and the Dutch 1,500.

The European traders operating in Dahomey during the seventeenth and eighteenth centuries were also active on the coast east of Lagos. The Bight of Benin and the Niger coastal delta region, known as the Oil Rivers, were much visited by traders from the various European countries. As elsewhere in Lower Guinea during the seventeenth and eighteenth centuries the slave trade was the main preoccupation of European traders and African middlemen in this region. As on the Dahomeyan coast the slave trade in Nigeria was conducted largely by individuals and small groups of traders. Practically no depots in the form of forts were built on the Nigerian coast. The European traders were able to move their vessels into the creeks and up the mouths of the rivers. The local chiefs and slave magnates saw to it that slaves were always ready in stock to be supplied to the slave vessels almost as quickly as they arrived. Mention ought to be made of Bonny in the great traffic of slaves on the West Africa coast, for it was undoubtedly the greatest exporter of slaves (mostly Ibos) on the whole coast in the last decades of the eighteenth century.

In the Bight of Biafra the Portuguese maintained their hold on the island of San Thomé long after they had withdrawn from most other parts of the Guinea Coast. However, they had their trying moments even on San Thomé. Towards the end of the sixteenth century, harassed by the French and the Dutch, many of the Portuguese colonists on the island emigrated to Brazil; even so, as many as 800 Europeans still continued to live on the island in addition to some 2,000 Creoles.

Questions

Chapter One

1. In what ways did the nature of the land affect historical developments in the Western Sudan?
2. Explain briefly how the Western Sudan was influenced by contacts with North Africa.
3. State the importance of the caravan routes linking the Western Sudan and North Africa.
4. How did the introduction of Islam affect the Western Sudan?
5. What is meant by the *Kisra Legend*? What is its significance in the history of the Western Sudan?
6. Explain the part played by the Zaghawa in the civilization of West Africa.
7. Assess the contribution of Arabic scholars to the written history of the Western Sudan.

Chapter Two

1. Why do you think the Tuareg should be considered important in the history of the Western Sudan?
2. 'The mystery people of West Africa'. Do you think this is a correct description of the Fulani?
3. Show the part played by the Mandingo or Mande-speaking peoples in the political and economic developments of West Africa.
4. Write briefly about the Chadic peoples or the inhabitants in the Lake Chad region during medieval times.

Chapter Three

1. How did medieval Ghana rise to fame in the Western Sudan?
2. What do we learn from El Bekri's accounts of the social and economic life of medieval Ghana?
3. Describe the territorial extent of the Ghana empire at the beginning of the eleventh century.
4. Assess the part played by the Almoravids in the decline of medieval Ghana.
5. What were the main achievements of Sundiata of Mali?
6. Describe Mansa Musa's great pilgrimage of 1324. How did it affect Mali?

7. Of what importance was Wangara to both Ghana and Mali?

Chapter Four

1. Show the stages by which Songhai rose to power by the middle of the fifteenth century.
2. Compare the methods by which Sonni Ali and Mohammed Askia made Songhai great.
3. How were the Mossi–Dagomba–Mamprusi kingdoms established? How did they differ from the great kingdoms to the north?
4. What part did Islam play in both Mali and Songhai?

Chapter Five

1. Why did El Mansur of Morocco plan the invasion of the Western Sudan?
2. Examine the parts played by Judar Pasha and Mahmud Pasha in the Moroccan invasion.
3. Explain the failure of Songhai resistance to the Moroccans.
4. Do you think the Moroccan invasion achieved its aims?
5. Discuss the permanent effects of the Moroccan invasion on the Western Sudan as a whole.

Chapter Six

1. Do you agree that the Lake Chad region was of special significance to the general history of West Africa during the medieval period?
2. How was the first Kanuri empire established? Why did it fall?
3. Discuss the internal organization of the kingdom of Bornu. How was the vast Bornu empire ruled?
4. How successful was the opposition to centralized Kanuri rule by the aboriginal tribes?
5. Assess the achievements of Idris Aloma as emperor of Bornu.
6. Show the importance of Islam in the civilization of Bornu.

Chapter Seven

1. How were the Hausa States formed?
2. Discuss the importance of Katsina and Kano as the leading city-states in Hausaland.
3. Describe briefly the main invasions of Hausaland from outside and show why the Hausas were unable to beat them off.
4. Explain the presence of the Fulani in Hausaland before 1800. What were their main grievances against Habe rule?

How was Islam introduced into Hausaland and what was its influence?

6. Account for the success of the Fulani *Jihad* of the early nineteenth century.

Chapter Eight

1. In what ways did the nature of the land affect the states of the southern region of West Africa?
2. Examine any possible links between the Western Sudan and the forest belt of West Africa.
3. Discuss the origin and establishment of the Yoruba states.
4. How did Oyo emerge as the dominant Yoruba kingdom?
5. How was the Oyo state organized and how did it rule its vast empire?
6. Account for the break-up of the Oyo empire in the course of the early nineteenth century.
7. What were the main aims for the expansion of Dahomey's authority during the eighteenth century? Why was this expansion successful?
8. Describe the internal organization of the kingdom of Dahomey and explain its main advantages.
9. Describe the position of the kingdom of Benin at the accession of Ewuare the Great. How did Ewuare further strengthen the kingdom?
10. Describe Benin City when the first Europeans visited it.
11. How was the kingdom of Benin administered?

Chapter Nine

1. Examine the accounts given of the origins of the Akan peoples.
2. How was the Bono state established and what lessons did it offer to Asante and the other later Akan states?
3. Explain briefly how Akwamu suceeded in building a large empire during the seventeenth century.
4. Account for the final overthrow of Akwamu.
5. How did Osei Tutu and Okomfo Anokye contribute to the greatness of Asante?
6. With what success did Opoku Ware continue the work of Osei Tutu?
7. On what rests the importance of Osei Kodjo in the history of Asante?
8. Why was Asante involved in war with the peoples of the coast in 1807? What were the results of the conflict?

Chapter Ten

1. Discuss the main points raised in connection with the origin of the Ibos.

2. Is it true to say that the Ibos lacked political organization?
3. Examine the Ibos' dealings with outsiders.
4. State briefly how Brass had become established by 1800.
5. Write brief notes on Kalabari, Bonny and Warri.
6. Outline the main effects of trade with Europeans on the states of the Niger delta.

Chapter Eleven

1. What were Prince Henry's main aims in organizing the Portuguese voyages to the West African coast? What preparations did he make?
2. Assess the progress of Portuguese exploration of the West African coast by 1482.
3. Discuss the challenge by other European nationals to the Portuguese claim of monopoly to the trade of the Guinea Coast. How successful was the challenge?
4. Discuss the development of trade on the Guinea Coast up to 1500.
5. How did the trans-Atlantic slave trade begin? How was it organized in general?
6. Examine the permanent effects of the slave trade on West Africa.
7. Describe the activities of the French in West Africa during the seventeenth and eighteenth centuries.
8. Why and how was the Crown Colony of Senegambia set up? Why did it fail?
9. Explain the difficulties in the way of the Colony of Sierra Leone up to 1808. How was total failure avoided?
10. Discuss the relations between English and Dutch on the Gold Coast during the seventeenth century.
11. Of what importance were the Dahomeyan and Nigerian coasts to the development of European trade during the seventeenth and eighteenth centuries?

For further reading

Part One
Ajayi, J. F. A. and Espie, I., A Thousand Years of West African History, Ibadan University Press, Nelson, 1965.
Bovill, E. W., Caravans of the Old Sahara, O.U.P., 1933; The Golden Trade of the Moors, O.U.P., 1958.

Davidson, Basil, *The African Past,* Longmans, 1954.
Ibn Batuta, *Travels in Asia and Africa, 1325–54,* trans. by H. A. R. Gibb, Routledge, 1957.
Mahmoud Kati, *Tarikh al Fattash,* trans. by Houndas O, Paris, 1915.
Murdock, G. P., *Africa: its Peoples and their Culture,* McGraw-Hill, 1959.
Seligman, C. J., *Races of Africa,* O.U.P., 1957.
Shaw, L. Flora, *A Tropical Dependency,* London, 1909.
Trimingham, J. S., *A History of Islam in West Africa,* O.U.P., 1962.

Part Two
Alagao, E. J., *The Small Brave City State: a History of Nembe-Brass in the Niger Delta,* Ibadan University Press, 1964.
Arnett, E. J., *The Rise of the Sokoto Fulani,* Kano, 1929.
Bacon, R. H., *Benin, the City of Blood,* London, 1897.
Barth, Heinrich, *Travels and Discoveries in Northern and Central Africa,* London, 1857.
Bello, Sir Ahmadu, the Sardauna of Sokoto, *My Life,* C.U.P., 1962.
Biobaku, S. O., *The Origin of the Yorubas,* Lagos, 1955.
Bradbury, R. E. and Lloyd, P. C., *The Benin Kingdom and the Edo-speaking Peoples of Nigeria,* International African Institute, 1957.
Buchanan, K. M. and Pugh, J. C., *Land and People in Nigeria,* University of London Press, 1955.
Burns, Sir Allan C., *History of Nigeria,* Allen & Unwin, Sixth Edition, 1963.
Crowder, Michael, *The Story of Nigeria,* Faber, 1962.
Davidson, Basil, *Old Africa Rediscovered,* Gollancz, 1959.
Egharevba, J. U., *A Short History of Benin,* Lagos, 1936.
Fage, J. D., *An Introduction to the History of West Africa,* C.U.P., Third Edition, 1962.
Forde, Daryll C., *The Yoruba-speaking Peoples of Southwestern Nigeria,* International African Instituto, 1061; *Efik Traders of Old Calabar,* International African Institute, 1956.
Fyfe, C., *A History of Sierra Leone,* O.U.P., 1962.
Herskovits, M. J., *Dahomey,* 2 Vols., New York, 1938.
Johnson, Samuel, *The History of the Yorubas,* Lagos, 1937.
Meek, C. K., *Northern Tribes of Nigeria,* O.U.P., 1925; *A Sudanese Kingdom,* Kegan Paul, 1931.
Oliver, R. and Fage, J. D., *A Short History of Africa,* Penguin Books, 1962.
Palmer, H. R., *The Bornu Sahara and Sudan,* Murray, 1936; *History of the first twelve years of the reign of Mai Idus Alooma of Bornu (1571–83) by his Imam, Ahmed Ben Faitua,* Lagos, 1926.

Priestley, M. and Wilks, I. G., 'The Ashanti Kings in the eighteenth century; a revised chronology', *Journal of African History,* Vol. 1, No. 1, 1960.

Robinson, C. H., *Hausaland,* London, 1896.

Roth, Henry L., *Great Benin: its Customs, Art and Honours,* Halifax, 1903.

Talbot, P. Amaury, *The Peoples of Southern Nigeria, Vol. I, Historical Notes,* O.U.P., 1926.

Thompson, Virginia and Adloff, Richard, *French West Africa,* Allen & Unwin, 1958.

Wilks, I. G., *The Northern Factor in Ashanti History,* University of Ghana, 1961; 'The Rise of the Akwamu Empire', *Transactions of The Historical Society of Ghana,* Vol. III, Part 2, 1957.

Index

The figures in italic refer to maps